from flicker To flame

from

flicker

to

flame

women's sermons for the
revised common lectionary

Year A

edited by Carole Ann Camp

Ash Grove Press

A percentage of every sale is contributed to groups and organizations which work toward creating a safe and healthy world.

Library of Congress Cataloging-in-Publication Data

Camp, Carole Ann.
  From Flicker to Flame: women's sermons for the revised common lectionary Year A, Volume 1: Advent to Pentecost.

Includes index.
ISBN: 1-886172-13-7
1. Religion. 2. Clergywomen. 3. Spirituality. 4. Sermons

Library of Congress Card Number: 94-73462

Printed in the United States of America
Cover Design by Lisa Carta

Is a trademark of Ash Grove Press, Inc.

Dedication

We Dedicate This Book To Women Prophets

—Past And Present—

Whose Voices Have Gone Unheard

Table of Contents

Table of Contents

Table of Contents

Acknowledgements

The Women of the Ash Grove wish to thank all of the people who have contributed their time and energy to this project. We especially want to thank the women whose sermons are included in this volume for sharing their insights and their understandings and interpretations of the Scriptual Lessons. This is the work of many hands and many hearts. We also wish to thank all those partners and friends who have encouraged and supported us on the way.

We are most grateful to Lisa Carta for designing the cover.

Introduction

It is with great excitement that we, the women of Ash Grove, present these two volumes of sermons by women. For those to whom the lectionary and the liturgical year are somewhat of a mystery, we offer this brief explanation.

The lectionary is a collection of fixed scriptural readings assigned for each Sunday throughout the church year. There are many different lectionaries. We have chosen to use the Revised Common Lectionary which was compiled by the Consultation on Common Texts and is in current use by many mainline denominations.

The Revised Common Lectionary is a three year cycle of Hebrew and New Testament readings. Worshippers in churches using these lectionary readings would hear approximately 95% of the New Testament and 60% of the Hebrew scriptures over the three year period. Each year one of the synoptic gospels is emphasized: Matthew in Year A, Mark in Year B, and Luke in Year C. Selections from John are read each year especially around Christmas, Lent, and Easter.

The church year contains the following seasons: Advent, Christmas, Epiphany, Lent, Easter, and Pentecost. Volume 1 of *From Flicker to Flame* contains sermons from Advent to Pentecost, and Volume 2 includes all the lessons for the season of Pentecost.

Most of the sermons in this collection are sermons that were actually preached in churches. We want to thank all of the clergywomen for sharing their thoughts and ideas, their hearts and their souls with us. We also want to thank our readers and editors who helped translate the spoken into the written word trying to follow the rules of the latter without damaging the essense of the former.

All scriptural texts are noted in the sermons with the exception of those directly from the day's lessons.

xiii

advent and christmas

Isaiah 2:1-5

Flicker Of Hope

Carole Ann Camp

Why the church leaders chose to begin the beginning of things in the last days of November is a mystery. It would make more sense to start the Christian year on Easter or even Pentecost. It is easier to metaphor beginnings of things with seeds and daffodils, the beginning of spring, warm summer breezes. But then those images really only work if you live north of the Equator, anyway. Historically, in the northern hemisphere, especially in northern European countries, people celebrated the winter solstice, the day of the year when there was the least amount of light. The celebrations evolved as a way to encourage the gods, especially the gods of the sun, to stop the darkness from overtaking the earth and to bring back the light. No one really knows when Jesus was born, so it was easy for the church leaders of the time to capitalize on an already established celebration, and they superimposed Christ's birth onto the winter solstice.

But what about Advent? Does it make any sense to have Advent start in late November? Whether by accident or design, the church calendar makers have, in fact, provided us with the most incredible metaphor of hope.

Every day as we go home from work, we notice that there is less and less light through which we can make our way. Every day we look out of our windows and it looks as if some artist has taken a color photograph and, by accident, developed it in black and white. The bright oranges and yellows have become

3

shades of gray. The trees have become naked, the garden bedraggled and scraggly.

Even our psyches go into depression. Feelings of loneliness stalk us. The number of suicides increases. Families hoping to become a Norman Rockwell painting become more and more dysfunctional. The homeless shelters pull out, from the summer closet, the signs that say, "Sorry, no more room." The old ones give up, and families stand huddled around frozen graves.

Why pick now to begin anything, especially the Christian year? Even the animals know better and have found some nice cozy hole where they can sleep it through. Yet here we are standing on the first day of the year. In which direction do we look? Any reasonable person can see that the darkness has a good chance of winning.

But wait! Far away on the very edge of our vision, God is lighting a candle. We can see it, if we look just right, if we squint our eyes just right. Dare we hope? Has God come through for us yet again?

Hope, desire with expectation. Hope, belief that it is obtainable.

The lesson for today promises us that the automatic assault weapons will be turned into tractors and plows, that the uzis will be turned into rakes and hoes.

When we read the newspapers, we have to wonder, when is all this going to happen? When will there be a time when peace and justice reign? Every day the number of poor and homeless increases. We dread watching the evening news because the atrocities of violence, people's inhumanity to other people, seem constant and without ceasing.

Flickers of doubt cross our minds. Will God's promise ever be fulfilled? Will the wolves ever dwell with the lambs? Will the calf and lion really play together? Will there ever come a time when people will not hurt or destroy any more? And will there ever come a time when the whole earth shall be full of the knowledge of God?

Is the prophesy of Isaiah just a bunch of empty promises? There are times when the dark is very dark. There are times when it feels like nothing is ever going to overcome all the hate and hurt, all the pain and violence, all the suffering and despair.

But God is lighting the candle of hope again and we see it. Barely maybe, but we see it. We know that even the tiniest flicker of one small candle can light up the whole world. Jesus is that light, that light that overcomes the pain and the struggle. Jesus is that light of hope.

When we get into this dark, cold, and dreary time of the year, the time of year when we might forget about God's promise, forget about Jesus in the midst of confusion and busyness, when we might think that despair and darkness may win out this year, the first candle is lit, this one small glimmer of hope. Timidly, it dances like a child in her first ballet recital.

There is another aspect to this dancing light that we should not forget. The darker the dark, the brighter this one little candle seems to shine. In a place of much light, the power of this one candle seems dimmed, maybe not even noticed. But as the darkness takes over, this candle comes into its power. It is in the hard times, when the light of one small candle makes the most difference.

That is our work. When the darkness starts to take over, we need to come into our power, too. It is in the hard times when the light of our hope makes the most difference. It is our work to hold God's dream alive. It is our work to remind the world, that we can have peace in our time. It is by our steadfastness to the vision of shalom, that the world may have that tiny flicker of hope.

Advent 2   Isaiah 11:1-10
                                            Matthew 3:1-12

One Crying In The Wilderness

Carol K. Towley

Who is the one crying in the wilderness, and who will prepare the way of the Lord?

As a child I was full of too much energy and very demanding. My father might have said that I was always crying in a wilderness where my wants and demands butted up against the boundaries and demands set in place by my parents. My mother might have said that she often felt like she was in a wilderness, trying to take care of house, home, children while her husband not only eked out a living, but a small fortune by the world's standards.

But at Christmas the real world ceased to exist. I was caught up in the promise: *You better watch out, you better not cry, you better not pout* (and I was a pouter), *I'm telling you why, Santa Claus is coming to town.*[1] I knew Santa was making a list, so about the first of November, when the first Christmas advertisements came out, I started being oh so good. I practiced smiling; I was even nice to my little brother. As the mountain of packages began to grow under the tree, I very secretly and carefully began pinching and shaking the gifts addressed to me, trying to decide which gift would be the one I would choose to open after the midnight Christmas Eve service. Boxes continued to arrive, cookies and breads were baked, fudge made, candles lit, and if there were any care in the world outside, I wasn't aware.

In 6th grade, we lived in California and my best friend was a boy from a Mexican family across the street. His house was smaller and more colorful than ours and there wasn't much in the way of furniture. But from his mother, I learned to make wonderful things out of boxes—doll houses, forts, storage cabinets, tables—several boxes taped together with a board on top and covered with a colorful cloth. And his house was always filled with wonderful smells and colorful bottles and pots filled with plants and flowers and pieces of paper and string. Not long after the beginning of school, his father was injured at work, and his mother took in ironing, but I didn't think about it much.

As Christmas approached, both our houses began to glow with Christmas magic—lights, trees, cookies, breads. And yet, as Christmas approached a nagging cloud seemed to develop and hang over our friendship. The presents under our tree grew and spilled out into the room. Under my friend's tree were the small presents we made at school—not much more.

Christmas Eve, just before we were leaving to go to church, my friend and his mother came to our house with a heaping plate of tamales and papier mache animals stuffed with peanuts and candy for my brother and me. My mother scrambled to put together a plate of cookies and fudge and holiday breads—a small dent in our mountain of plenty. I cried that night and my father said that I was becoming more aware of the world around me—I was becoming aware of the wilderness and I wasn't sure that such awareness was a good thing.

Who is the one crying in the wilderness, and who will prepare the way of the Lord?

Later, in high school, my best friend told me that she hated Christmas. Most of the time just her father drank, but at

Christmas everyone drank. Things got broken, words were spoken, people's space and personhood were violated in gross and subtle ways. At the time, I chose not to be aware of the fear and pain around me. Not that I didn't care, I just didn't know what to say or do. We had our worst fight just before Christmas and our friendship seemed shattered and peace on earth seemed like a cruel joke.

Who is the one crying in the wilderness, and who will prepare the way of the Lord?

As a young mother, I wanted to recreate the Christmas magic I felt as a child. In a time of Viet Nam, campus riots, the death of my uncle, we limited our conversation to love, giving, lights, candy, presents, Santa, mulled cider and the Christ child, trying to create a world that was, just for a moment, close to the perfection that I thought God willed. I didn't want to see, and I didn't want my children to see, the awful reality of the world as it was—not at Christmas.

But one year, my sons said, "This is stupid, we know the stories by heart, let's just open the presents." And suddenly, I was in the wilderness that we all knew, but of which no one spoke. Our family was unraveling and full of anger and even the magic of Christmas couldn't cover or erase the hurt, the fear, the betrayal. We were the ones crying in the wilderness of our own making. Who would prepare the way of the Lord?

What was being prepared? Why was John calling people to repent and to be baptized? Why did John call the Pharisees and Sadducees, who came to repent and be baptized, a brood of vipers and unworthy of repentance?

I'm not sure I know the answer for others, but for myself I know that until I experienced my own personal wilderness, I just didn't get it. My heart knew to cry when my poor friend brought us a plate of tamales, and my spirit was uneasy when my friend told me about the horrors of Christmas at her house. But to acknowledge poverty, abuse, loneliness, violence and to not know what to do to make it different, is to risk feeling powerless and incompetent.

Who is the one crying in the wilderness, and who will prepare the way of the Lord?

Eric Hoffer said in his book *The True Believer:*

> When hopes and dreams are loose in the streets, it is well for the timid to lock doors, shutter windows and lie low until the wrath has passed. For there is often a monstrous incongruity between the hopes, however noble and tender, and the action which follows them. It is as if ivied maidens and garlanded youth were to herald the four horsemen of the apocalypse.[2]

The work of Christmas is not the lovely play of lights, good smells, presents, and food baskets for the poor. It is the work of risking to see each other as we really are—lonely, hurt, afraid, hungry, in need of love and forgiveness that God offers; and it is the work of risking to see the world as it really is—caught in a struggle for power, wealth, land, influence, votes—a world so caught in the mechanics of survival that people, individuals, get overlooked and stepped on.

Advent means *parousia*, arrival, coming—it is both the present and future. The Messiah whose advent we celebrate and expect is a reviver of the ancient promise to the Davidic dynasty. He is an agent of God's deliverance. He is the apocalyptic son of God. He is a political, ethical, apocalyptic savior. To understand or to act on only one meaning of Advent and the coming Messiah, is to be lost in the wilderness.

Many, like Judas, expected Jesus to be a political savior, the one who would lead the army of Israel to conquer the Romans and return Israel to its rightful position in the world. But Christ accepts every applicant, and his army is full of rag-tag, barefoot, maimed, sick, poor, uneducated, brilliant, unable to march, afraid to shoot a gun, people of all ages and backgrounds. Judas was right when he saw Jesus as a man of power, but he mistook the power of the Cross for military might.

For some, Christ's saving power is yet to come and they await the end of the world and Christ's second coming. This divine intervention would come at the end of history. It would mark the end of human free will as God finally, in the twinkling of an eye, perfected the world according to God's will. God would use power to force people to act according to God's will.

To Amos and some of the later Old Testament prophets, the Messiah would bring an ethical revolution. The Messiah would herald the day when the eyes and hearts of the people would be opened; a day when we would choose to be God's people. A day when our love of the Lord would turn our hearts around, and we would treat one another fairly and follow the Golden Rule; a day when the poor would share their original inheritance; a day when all debt would be forgiven, prisoners set free, slaves freed, and widows comforted.

> A shoot shall come out from the stump of Jesse, and a branch shall grow out of his roots. The spirit of the Lord shall rest on him . . . and the wolf shall live with the lamb, and the leopard shall lie down with the kid, the calf and the lion and the fatling together and a little child shall lead them

> . . . They will not hurt or destroy on all my holy mountain;
> for the earth will be full of knowledge of the Lord as the
> waters cover the sea.

Who is the one crying in the wilderness, and who will prepare the way of the Lord?

Perhaps I should be asking what is the wilderness? And why do I assume it is a bad place? Perhaps my own discomfort with my own wilderness has blinded me to the Biblical history of God calling a people into the wilderness. Perhaps it is our wilderness experiences that opens our eyes, hearts, and minds to God's will and promise. Perhaps this Advent, instead of trying to recreate a lovely light-filled, present-filled oasis of perfect love, harmony, and unawareness, we should open our ears to the ones crying in the wilderness. We will discover that it is us that God is calling—Prepare ye the way of the Lord.

Preparation begins with a willingness to see the world as it is, with a willingness to change. Action is made possible by the strength and power and hope of the Holy Spirit and by the promise that God is a God of mercy and righteousness who will not leave us a dispirited, homeless, scattered people. This Advent, John again calls us from our comfort and our plenty. John again reminds us that this time and in this place we are the voice, the hands, the love, the word of hope and of forgiveness. We must take seriously the preparing of our own hearts, our own churches, our own organizations, our own communities, for the word and the hope of salvation to be heard. If we write on the doorposts of our churches: WELCOME, ALL WHO ARE BEATEN, DEPRESSED, DISCOURAGED, DEFEATED! THE GOD OF HOPE AWAITS YOU HERE, let us be prepared to make it come true.

Advent 3

Isaiah 35:1-10
Luke 1:47-55
Matthew 11:2-11

Unexpected Joy Available

Mary E. Giles

Today we continue our journey through Advent. The excitement continues to build. Our lives continue to be busy, too busy perhaps. We are reminded how many shopping days are left before Christmas. We make plans with friends and family. We decorate our homes and attend more open houses. And the stress may be building.

This third Sunday in Advent is also known as Rejoice Sunday or Joy Sunday. There is the mood of joyful anticipation of the coming Savior. There is the excitement that has been bottled up and held in. We have contained it so long, and now it is about to burst into our midst. What happened to our patience?

Today we are being called to recall what this season is about. We are being called to experience the transforming joy of God's gift to us. But I believe that we are also being called to remember that this is not a happy time for everyone. This can be one of the loneliest times of the year for some. It can be painful. Some can only recall the death of a loved one. There are many who feel the pain of strained family relationships. Some single people feel the pressure of a culture that insists that you must be in relationship to be whole. And there are those in "nontraditional" families who are constantly bombarded with the expectations of the traditional nuclear family as the only way to be.

It can be difficult to find the joy that is available, that seems to be hidden for many. We need to take their pain and ours seriously, bringing it to God in prayer, in confession, in attentiveness. And we need to continue the journey, living into the images of hope offered in this season of the unexpected.

Our reading from Isaiah has a mood of joy; joy that comes in unexpected ways. Here are exiles returning home through the desert. And the desert has been transformed into a highway toward home, a highway filled with blossoms and with abundant water. This is a wonderful image. It is an image one can also see in the northern tundra. One day everything seems plain and barren and virtually lifeless. The next, the area is filled with bloom, with color, with life. Everything is growing like crazy. And if we close our eyes to it, if we stand in the desert or the tundra and choose to ignore it, we will miss the unexpected riot of joy, of color, of new life.

Can you hear the piece of Advent in this? We are preparing. We are waiting. We are getting ready. But let's not miss it. Jesus is coming in an unexpected way. And if we choose to miss it all, if we choose to close our eyes and our hearts, if we choose to ignore the hidden and unexpected gifts that are there for us, we'll find ourselves back in the dry desert or the barren tundra. We will miss the hope, and we will miss the joy that is available.

Our Gospel lesson today gives us a continuing look at John the Baptist, one who was waiting and looking for signs of God's coming realm. And he had questions about Jesus. Jesus didn't meet John's expectations of a leader, of a Messiah. We sometimes have trouble listening to this austere sounding preacher named John. But we need to hear him. He is not gentle. Perhaps he wouldn't be considered very pastoral in today's church. His words can sound quite harsh and condemning to us. Yet there are many among us who are far more ready to hear the condemnation than a call to joyful living. We are too ready to hear the pain or the guilt without listening for something else, something more. We know too well how to feel guilty. We are less sure how to feel joyful.

I love being with children who haven't yet been taught to suppress their feelings of joy. While I was attending a junior high concert, I had a delightful time watching a couple of youngsters sitting nearby. They were moving their bodies with the music. And they were imitating the conductor, waving their arms. This soon turned into a moving and spinning dance to the music. As one of them spun around, I saw the joyful twinkle in his eyes. And I began to think about how he was expressing joy. Can we allow ourselves to express joy? Can we express the joy of our faith with our whole body, with our whole lives, with our whole being?

I wish we could be more easily open to the unexpected joys that can tickle us if we allow them into our being. And I wish we would express our joy more so that it could multiply. What would it be like if we expressed our joy more openly in the church, the genuine joy that is expressed by children? Why do we sit here in church with sober and serious faces? Can we truly hear the phrase "Rejoice in the Lord always, again I say rejoice!" (Philippians 4:4) and just sit still and be passive?

I am reminded of my experiences in the Pentecostal Church of Chile. The worship experience there is one where people DO express their joy. They sing, they dance, they clap, they shout, they move. They express the joy of their faith in very real ways.

Their lives may be hard, many have very little material wealth, tragedy has struck their families but they are open to unexpected joys and they express the joy of their faith and, in that, they find the courage and the grace to continue.

We talk about peace and grace and forgiveness. But we can't know these gifts except as they come through the sense of joy. We talk about a rational, logical world, but if we aren't careful, we will miss the irrational and illogical promises of God's love which bring us hope and joy.

Mary finds herself pregnant in a situation far from ideal. In the context of her culture, her pregnancy means she could be ostracized and perhaps killed. Yet she senses the new life growing within her, and she senses the possibility of a world where the hungry will be fed and the lowly lifted up. She had no logical reason to think this way, no facts on which to base her hope. Yet she accepts this gift of life and of hope in her body and in Elizabeth's body, and she sings out her call for justice as she sings out her joy. It is illogical. It is irrational. It is unexpected. But it is real. It is joy.

I have tried unsuccessfully to find a good definition of joy. Perhaps joy is something that can't be caught in words. But it can be experienced. And it can be experienced in situations which are decidedly not happy. It can be experienced sitting with a dying family member. It can be experienced in the midst of grinding poverty. It can be known in the dark of a cold night in a war-torn land.

Joy is not something we experience by ignoring pain and loudly singing, "Everything's coming up roses."[3] It is easy to focus on the pain or on the dying or on the strained relationships. But we can choose to be open to joy even in the midst of it all. We can choose to be open to the unexpected, the illogical, the irrational. We can choose to hear the voice of God over all the noise. We can choose to see the flowers in the desert.

We have a choice. We can choose to live in fear, in doubt, in pain, in prejudice. The situation in which we find ourselves doesn't matter as much as how we choose to be in it, how we choose to deal with it, how we choose to live with the people we are with. We can choose to live with hope, with understanding, with love, being open to the unexpected joy that is available to us. We can make that choice by knowing ourselves and knowing that God loves us, and so rejoice with God. We can tap into the oasis of joy even when we don't feel joyful. We can be open to the transformation that joy brings, when we choose it.

This is the season we prepare for and celebrate Christ's coming. Christ's coming is transformative, and if we wish to know the joy and peace of God's transformation, we need to open ourselves now to a new world—a world in which power is shared and all have what they need, a world where people can live in relationship, in celebration, in joy. As we recognize the brokenness of our world, we can also recognize the unexpected joys. And this will allow us to continue to work for justice and peace in our world and in how we choose to live in our world. And we can live into the image of healing hope and joy and wholeness. Let's be open to joy.

Advent 4   Matthew 1:18-25

Rumors And Angels

Nancy Rockwell

"Angels can fly," says the old Scottish proverb, "because they take themselves lightly."

No one I know takes angels lightly, though. Most people I know don't take angels at all, being unaccustomed to their presence in the everyday imagination. We are inarticulate about such things as angels. It would stop the conversation at any Christmas cocktail party if someone were to say, "I saw an angel yesterday and heard—" Nonetheless we people Christmas with them, cards and crèches and tree ornaments and pageants, all displaying angels we take reverently, soberly, advisedly. I've never, ever heard an angel joke.

What we take lightly, of course, is Mary, poor old thing. She's been the butt of endless jokes for centuries. Small boys snigger about her ("I can believe it if Joseph could"), and grown men roll their eyes ("religion is believing what you know to be untrue"). Theologians either denigrate or venerate her, all on the basis of her virginity, disregarding, for purposes of theological merit, her pluckiness, her stamina, her survival skills, her determination (shown more and more as Jesus gets older), her willingness to march to a different drummer, and her recorded argument with an angel, something only Abraham, Jonah and Gideon had done before her.

18

All those sniggers, I think, have nothing to do with her and everything to do with relations between the rest of us. What we take lightly is really of serious importance to us.

No one fusses about the rest of the miracles in the Christmas story. Stars can guide wise men, wise men can find stables and leave precious gifts; angels can visit, talk, sing in the heavens; shepherds, kings and Joseph can have their miracles; without anybody raising a fuss. It's only Mary's miracle that has us shouting humbug! She's the one whom we don't want to have special attention at Christmas.

It isn't the child we're trying to demote. He can have his gold, frankincense and myrrh, his star, his visitors, his harrowing escape from Herod. But she'd better not try any of that. Where babies come from and who makes decisions about them is a deadly earnest issue in our times.

Of course, most of us Protestants are in a constant state of reaction to the Catholics, who take Mary's miracle out of the context of the story of a whole people experiencing divine possibility, and make Mary's miracle a religion all by itself. Then she gets used to keeping all the rest of the women in the world in line. A fine miracle that is!

Well, that's where angels come in. Literally, in the story. Here comes the angel, offering Mary an opportunity, a possibility, if she's willing to undertake it. It's an awful lot of work, two thousand years so far, and still people are sniggering away. But she accepts the challenge. Bravo for her!

Angels, you see, don't help people out at all, though that is their reputation. Neither do angels make things happen or keep things from happening. What they do is announce possibilities. And the rest is up to us.

"This baby could be here, but it's up to you, Mary."

"King Herod could get this baby, unless you go home some other way, Wise Men."

"This woman could have to go through this all alone, unless you, Joseph, choose to trust her."

Angels don't offer people comfort. They offer people challenges. Angels offer people the opportunity to leave the relative comfort of their own lives and take on the tremendous discomfort of bringing a new possibility into the world, into other people's lives. Which is, I think, the way the Holy always enters into our situation. Time and time again, that is the way. Ordinary people move beyond themselves, move into a territory that is uncharted, risk finding their way by following stars (how foolish!) or by raising children the world doesn't approve of, or even by being saddled with the moniker Holy Virgin.

A possibility. That's all the angels offer. You have to figure out how to make it happen. You have to find a way to get through the difficulties and obstacles that surround you and make the possibility depend on you. You, on your own, depending on your wits and your courage and your commitment.

So Mary had to figure out how to make a a relationship with Joseph—now! And Joseph had to figure out where she could have this baby in Bethlehem. And then he had to figure out how they could survive in Egypt, and when to come back to Nazareth. And Mary had to figure out what every mother strives to learn—how to raise a child who has enough wisdom and enough courage to answer his own angels.

The hallmarks of angels seem to be this: what they offer will get you laughed at by your friends, and strangers, too. You'll never be able to get back to your own agenda. You won't gain wealth or glory. You will hurt, and often. It will be the most wonderful thing you've ever done. Probably angels are offering these possibilities to us all the time.

The real miracle of Christmas, then, is that so many people said yes to their angels that The Possibility was able to live a long time, at least long enough for the world to notice or remember. Think how many holy possibilities may have gone unnoticed in the world because shepherds somewhere turned over and went back to sleep, or because searching wise ones gave up the quest before they had gone far enough, before they had checked out even the stable floors.

Here are some of the people we have seen in our lifetime who have accepted the offers of their angels, and kept Holy Possibilities alive, in extraordinary ways, until we noticed and remembered: Nelson Mandela; Albert Schweitzer; Vaclav Havel; Mother Theresa. They've all been sniggered at. And they've each called themselves blessed, and servants of something larger than themselves.

The angels have winged their way over our little town, too, challenging people here to extraordinary acts.

There's Abby, who has spent the last few years working with tribal people to save James Bay—she even celebrated her eightieth birthday among them! And there's Eliot, who has spent decades working with the NAACP Legal Defense Fund, making a dream of justice a real and honored possibility. And there's Priscilla, who leaves Lincoln every day to spend eight or ten hours or more working out alternative sentencing for women in the Boston Court system. And there's Herb, who was an international agribusinessman, comfortable in the upper circles, and who gave it all up to become a nurse in a clinic for Mexican migrant worker children. All these friends have heard the sniggers. And they've heard the angels. And they know the real joy of great blessing.

Angels are everywhere. Christmas is the time to speak about their tidings and their offerings to us. May we all find our way to Bethlehem, where wonder is forever, and a lot of endless jokes are born!

Christmas 1   Matthew 2:13-23

Fear After Christmas

Donna Schaper

Children are not supposed to be afraid. And mothers are not supposed to be afraid. And fathers are not supposed to be afraid.

But some children have awful nightmares. And some mothers know the table is too thinly laid, sometimes even when it has a lot of food on it. And some fathers drive on tires so thin and brakes so worn that they know they get places because of angels and not because of wheels.

Which is why, right after Christmas Eve, the first story is always about fear and flight. The reason we like the story so much is that it counsels us not to fear. "Fear not, For Behold." The power of the story is that it guarantees that there is no reason to be afraid. And does so in the name of Jesus Christ.

Sometimes we are more impressed by the problems of the world than by the power of God. Sometimes we think that everything depends on us, a thought guaranteed to make us depressed. But in this season we remember that everything is up to God. There are men chasing children everywhere, but they are not catching them. Finally, they will be stopped by the power of God.

The same Herods are also after what remains of the child in us, too. Our adult souls get slowly bent-out-of-shape by their too eager embrace of dishtowel and broom, their love affair with the ratchet wrench, their assumption that if we just get enough stuff surrounding us we will be protected against the Herods.

It is as though we have looked in a mirror and seen ourselves in a funny shape. A bent out of shape circus shape that said that we are empty inside and need cultural filling.

The truth is the opposite of this distortion. What is good about us is what is inside, what is God-given, what exists despite effort or wealth, how we are, in fact, the image of God. When the angel said, "Be not afraid," what she meant to do was to evoke that inner strength against outer distortion. Angels wipe out fear by recasting the mirror of ourselves. The spirit recasts the mirror.

That reversal of distortion includes your childhood and my childhood. And that new curious thing called our inner child. Forgive the jargon. I couldn't help it. And the word is popular for very good reason. There are a lot of us so tied to our mortgages and our dishtowels that we have forgotten how to play.

The modern Herods are also killing the modern children with the conspiracy to make them happy. To fill their ears with the distortion that things and effort produce happiness. John Updike thought of America as a vast conspiracy to make people happy. God knows, we work at it. And wouldn't it be fun not to work at it for awhile? To give up all the effort of making happy and just be it or do it. Dishtowels folded and put away, us in the living room eating popcorn we don't have to clean up later.

We have forgotten that Herod ultimately loses, and the child is saved and goes on to save us.

The worst mistakes I ever made in my life were because I was afraid. I didn't listen to the angels, but instead, listened to the dishtowels. Or the bills. And, at the same time, the worst mistakes I ever made in my life were because I wasn't careful enough. Get the problem? You and I will make mistakes because we are not afraid enough or because we are too afraid. We have to take some risks to be happy. One is to make sure that the great conspiracy requiring happiness doesn't catch hold of our credit card. Another is to risk knowing who we are rather than knowing our distortions. A third is to make mistakes willingly, freely, as though they were expected guests.

A wise person said, "Even if you're on the right track you can still get run over if you just stay still." It is important to respect fear. To understand that it is a very real threat to our human existence.

We don't understand Christmas by looking at the sunny side of God. We don't get to understand what the carol means when it says to "Fall on your knees, O hear the angel voices" [4] if we don't take our human fears very, very seriously. There are powerful people chasing children. They mean to kill them if they catch them. They mean to kill you if they catch you. But we begin to see what it means if we understand that Christmas comprehends the dark side, is chased by Herod, and still says, "Fear, not, for behold."

The power of God is greater than the power of evil. That's the reason we're singing. That's the reason we can choose spaciousness over stinginess even if our brakes are shot or our table too thinly laid.

And the angel said to her, "Be not afraid." Don't think for a minute that the angel didn't see Herod. She said, "Don't be afraid" without distortion. She knew exactly what Herod was up to. And she also knew what God was up to. God is going to take us home by another road, one that will out-pace Herod and all his hellions. Christmas is an invitation to get on that road and stay there. To not get detoured by our fear. Or by the very real Herods of the world.

Or the very real Herods inside us.

We are free to fear. But free in an ever larger way. When we get over "the supposed to be," the way children and mothers are not supposed to be afraid, we shake hands with Herod. The Herod outside. The Herod inside. And then we go beyond. Our faith hears what the angels say. "Fear not." We make our lives have meaning with fear, not without it. We go beyond Herod. We don't let him get in our way for long.

Christmas 2   John 1:1-18

And The Word Became Flesh

Donna Schaper

The Word became flesh in so many ways, at so many times, that it learned its way very well. Now we can simply keep our eyes and ears open and watch it wend its way. God became Jesus. Divinity became humanity. Eternity took a taste of time. Big, universal became small and particular.

What follows are a few stories about how words can take on flesh to reveal Jesus. The admonition of this text is that we become such good students of our own experience that we are always watching for sightings of the Christ.

He may come in psychotherapy. Or in turnips. Or in whatever other strange thing builds our life today. We are simply to watch for the promise to come true. The Word will become flesh and dwell among us.

I think of a child who I spoke to the other day in a Thrift Shop. He was talking about what it had been like to be with his father and his brothers and sisters in the shelter since his mother died two years ago. He talked about watching his father learn to sew. About watching him learn to braid his sister's hair. Then he said something that startled me. "I tried to sell my Nintendo to get some money to help out, but nobody would buy it." The news that we can have what we let go of became real. The child learned the Christmas spirit that can't be bought.

The Word became flesh.

A father reports having spent thousands of dollars on therapy for his four year old son. The child wouldn't obey him; the child was out of control.

The father was mature enough to know that it wasn't just the son's problem, that no doubt he played some important part in the problem.

Finally, one day, in a spurt of anger at the child who would not clean up his room, the father began to throw all the stuffed animals from the floor onto the child's bed. The child jumped on the bed and began to throw them out with equal vigor. The father threw them back. The son threw them off.

They went on like this for a few minutes until the boy began to laugh gleefully. He was having a ball, playing this game with his father. The pair ritualized the game. They play it now at least once a day and always as soon as the father comes home from work. The child has become more cooperative, the father happy, and the family more content.

The therapist was shocked that such a simple act of play resolved whatever battle of wills existed between the parent and child. But we who understand Bethlehem are not one bit surprised. We know the power of the little things.

The news that we get control by letting go of control became real.

The Word became flesh.

The meaning of Christmas survives because of Bethlehem. If it had been set in Jerusalem or had a larger press budget, it would have long been gone. Christmas is an annual people's revolt, showing how small things matter in a world where big is king. Advent is the preparation for the Word to become flesh in Jesus, at Bethlehem.

Because we bet on Bethlehem over Jerusalem, we expect the small to be standing when the large trips. We expect words of hope to become real.

Bethlehem confirms what we already know. Getting new tires for the car can be as cumbersome as waging world peace. The same people who battle for years against cancer can be thrown by a bad flu bug. If the little things can really get to us, why would they not also have positive power? A big word, love, became a small human who flesh-framed the world.

Christmas exposes the irony of scale. Valleys are exalted and mountains are brought low. Little things begin, in that great cliché, to mean a lot.

I mentioned even turnips as vehicles for the flesh of God. A two ton truckload of turnips arrived at my church in New York one year, the day before Christmas. Brad Reeve, a local farmer, donated them to our soup kitchen. A lot of people would like to have left them right there. Send Mr. Reeve a nice, gracious note, thanking him for the turnips, the delivery of the turnips, the dumping out of the turnips on church property, and hope that he never does anything like that again.

When the truckload of turnips arrived, the word sort of went out around town. One of the soup kitchen's regular clients, a man who often showed up un-inebriated, showed up inebriated. For him Christmas Eve started early and ended much, too much, later. He took one look at the enormous pile of turnips, laying there inert on cold ground, said, "Oh man, they said you had food over here. All you got is turnips."

His comment reminds me for all the world of an average supper at our house. They said you had food here—all you got is peas.

And, we have to tell our children, what we got is good.

People don't feed each other with words only. They also feed each other with food. And if all "you got" is turnips, then they become part of your word.

There is a wonderful poem called *Jacob*. It goes like this:

Years and scars later
I finally realized
That all angels
Travel under assumed names.[5]

All angels travel under assumed names. Sometimes they come as peas, other days as turnips, sometimes as cascading stuffed animals, sometimes as Nintendos. The angels are not going to switch their habit. Their habit is not to be habitual. Their regularity is the way they come in irregular ways. Their orthodoxy is their unorthodoxy. Years and scars later, we must teach our children that all the angels travel under assumed names.

I don't care if you like turnips or not. What I do care about is marvel. We just have to have some people around who can marvel. Everybody doesn't have to marvel all the time. Some people are legitimate when they say, THEY said you have food over here, all you got is turnips. Some people are correct when they inquire as to who allowed them to dump a load of turnips on the church lawn. Children are right about some of the meals we serve them. Every time the word becomes flesh, it is not as pretty as a baby in a manger.

But some have to be open to marvel, or at least to wishful thinking. Wishful thinking tries to discover which angel is traveling beside us and which of her assumed names she is using today. The angel turnip? The angel pea? The angel Gabriel?

The angel Brad Reeve? The angel generosity? The angel marvels . . . as she bends down on Christmas Eve and loads turnips at twilight into the soup kitchen accompanied by dozens of drunks and just a few very sober people. Do come, all ye faithful. The turnips are on.

The Word of God is becoming the flesh. Here. Now.

Ask Ulysses, the seminarian. One balmy night about seven o'clock, when he went to the door of his church, early in his Miami internship, he heard what he thought were firecrackers. He entered the church vestibule only to be grabbed by a woman and dragged out on to the street where another woman lay bleeding. She had been shot in the head by a drive-by shooter. Her two children, ages four and seven were leaning down over her yelling, "Mommy, Mommy wake up, Mommy." It was clear that she was already dead. He reports that he put his arms around the children in the street and called out the name of God. He reports feeling like a shelter, a useless shelter but feeling that there was nothing to do but to sit there and hold on to the children. The police came. The ambulance came. The reporters came. It was when the reporters came that Ulysses remembered who he used to be. An observer. Now, he reported, as he sat there in the middle of a street in the middle of Miami, sheltering two children not his own, now he was no longer an observer. He had become something useless like a shelter. Maybe even a minister.

The Word became flesh, in him, in his arms, in a way that would never reverse itself.

The Saturday before Christmas we had in a group of friends. They all brought "extras," mothers visiting for the holidays, recently divorced associates, odd ones out. In the middle of the party the children staged a floor show. It was typical of their floor shows in its want of beginning, middle and end. But costumes it had. And music it had. And, surprise! They had brought in the bunny from its cage, put it in a hat, and, right in the middle of the season of drama and fantasy, popped a real bunny out of a real hat.

Afterwards Jacob came running down the hallway yelling at Isaac, "Give me back my eyeball."

There are so many times when all we have are disorganized stories. No plot. Absurdist dialogue. Disconnected characters. A longing for the magic of a *deus ex machina*. When all we can do is play our part, and live by the faith that Word will become flesh, that our stories will take on plot.

And the Word will become flesh in us.

Most of life forces us to impossible conclusions. Much of life also tries to bring people down. To make us smaller. I think of the Simpson family game, a new board game in which all the Simpsons are at each other's throats as rivals. The object is for each player's character to sabotage the other's accomplishments—along the way they engage in a burping contest. Sounds a lot like the modern office. Or corporation. Or church. How to make ourselves look bigger by making other people look smaller.

And the Word becomes flesh to connect our stories. To organize their plots. To move us beyond the need for competition.

Despite the flimsy plot, the naive hopes, the competitions, the oppressions, we are all connected. Our arms still wind round each other. No matter how buried some of the love. Give me back my eyeball, I might pray. So I can begin to see the connections.

So that the Word become flesh can be fresh in me. So that I may value the smallness of my own Bethlehem and know that it too, is the large word of God concretizing, in-corporating, becoming flesh.

Epiphany

Epiphany

Isaiah 42:1-9
Matthew 2:1-12

New Things I Now Declare

Mary Clark Moschella

January 6 is the day Christians call "epiphany," meaning, the manifestation of God to the Magi. We commemorate the particular manifestation God used to guide the Magi—the star that guided them to Bethlehem to see the Christ child. We remember this epiphany wherein the star became a sign of God.

What really happened? We can't possibly know, except to say that there was a moment one starry night, when the sacred and the mundane collided, or colluded, taking the form of light. Ancient Chinese astronomers record that in the year 5 B.C.E., the planet Venus traveled seventy-six days on the horizon as the morning star of the East. In trying to date the birth of Jesus, some have speculated that our Christian calendar is about five years off, and that the eastward moving planet Venus was the "star" that the wise men followed, coinciding with the birth of Jesus. This is an explanation that will appeal to some of us, those like my three year old son, who always needs to know exactly how things work. "How do babies get born, Mommy?" he asks. "Head first," I answer, dodging. "No," he calls me back to task, "I want to know, where's the place for the baby to come out?" Some of us need to know the scientific explanations, the precise nature of events. And yet, when it comes to the stories of our faith, we can't always get the blunt answers we seek. The origins of Matthew's infancy narrative are complex and

37

fascinating, no doubt a mixture of tradition, faith, and imagination. The important point about the story is that God's light came flashing headlong across the sky, and three star-gazers caught a glimpse.

The power of the passage comes through to us most clearly, in the image of the star, the mystical, magical light, used by God to guide the wise ones to Christ. Light is a particularly appropriate sign of God for us, as we begin the New Year in the darkness of winter, enlivened by the lengthening days and renewed by the hope of our various resolutions. Light and newness intermingle as we hear the words of Isaiah: "Behold, the former things have come to pass, and new things I now declare."

How is it that God lights our path? How do we experience the epiphany? What are the stars that guide us? Last spring, I experienced a sense of epiphany through an unusual series of events. I had been searching for professional renewal, and decided to attend a course in writing. It was a weekend course in Portland, Maine. On the way, I stopped in the Boston area to see an art opening, the work of a dear friend. The woman coordinating the show began to talk of her travels around the world, how she worked on barges to earn her passage to Alaska; how she lived the adventure from day to day. Then she said a curious thing: she said that upon entering each new country, each new city, when she got off the plane or the bus or the boat, she would look for the direction of the light. She would walk in that direction, until she got her bearings, and settled into the new place.

As I drove into Portland that day, I remembered the woman's words about following the light. I decided to approach the city as if I were a world traveler. A little lost, I parked my car and started walking toward the afternoon light. I found a bookstore/cafe and settled in with a cup of herbal tea. I was startled to look up to see an old friend. She was herself supposed to be traveling around the world. I'd just gotten a postcard from Kenya. What was she doing back in Portland? A brief but rich conversation followed. The coincidence was uncanny; the light had brought us together.

Events such as these may seem rare. How often does the light of God really reach us and break through into our mundane lives? Or maybe the light is always there, but it's only rarely that we notice. Elizabeth Barrett Browning writes "Earth's crammed with heaven, And every common bush a fire with God. But only he who sees, takes off his shoes."[1] Maybe we need to take off our shoes more often. Maybe we need a little more reverence for the moment, or a little more time outside, staring at the stars.

Were you ever in a situation where you weren't quite sure what to do, yet you felt a little tugging, a little intuitive nudging in one direction or another? I find this happens quite a lot, but it isn't always easy to trust the feeling, or to heed the twinkle of wisdom that flashes across the screen. Yet some of our best insights and creative impulses come to us that way. You'll be working on a really tough problem, going at it like a bull, trying to solve it directly. You see you're getting nowhere, so you put it aside and go do something else. Then later that night, as you're bathing the children or doing the dishes, suddenly, it hits you: the solution you were looking for earlier, the missing piece to the puzzle.

The creative processes of our thinking and of our human experience of God sometimes surprise us. Does the Spirit move through our thoughts and emotions? I hope so. Annie Dillard

claims that we "come at God with an unwarranted air of profes-
sionalism, with authority and pomp, as though [we] knew what
[we] were doing."[2] In reality we're all following hunches in the
religious life. We're dancing in the dark. We're searching for
stars.

There's a trickiness to this business of epiphanies. It's not as
if we can be on a quest for one. We can't create the light, but
we can try to put ourselves in the path. We can't force epiphanies. But we don't want to miss them, either.

My sense is that we're all granted plenty of light, numerous
ways and occasions to look into the face of the divine. There's
something about the new year that brings us all a certain amount
of clarity and insight. The stark newness of time hails the hope
for a brighter, better year. We don't have to think hard to come
up with resolutions; they veritably suggest themselves. The need
to clean one's desk, for example. One has to clear away yesterday's clutter in order to make room for the new things, the new
thoughts, the new ideas that need space of their own. Another
popular resolution has to do with diet and exercise. We want to
be healthy and fit to face the New Year. Maybe this will be the
year to write that novel or plant that garden. Maybe this is the
time for new things, new ways of being in the world.

Now what, you may ask, does this have to do with God?
Does God really care about such things? Isn't God concerned
with loftier matters, things having to do with justice and peace
or at least personal piety? Yes and no. Of course God is concerned with justice and peace. And God certainly wouldn't be
opposed to a New Year's resolution to attend church regularly.
But no, God is not limited to the grander causes. Holiness per-
vades life. God is in the small matters, too. And resolving to

fulfill dreams and goals is not necessarily a small matter. If your heart yearns to plant a garden maybe that is your spiritual discipline; maybe that will be the path of God's light to you. And if your goal is to get along better in your family, this will add to peace in the world. God can work in and through it all.

Doug and I spent New Year's Eve with his best friend, Dick Blake, and his family in their parsonage in Highland Park, New Jersey. The excitement of the occasion was enhanced by the fact that it was also Dick's fortieth birthday. We had a marvelous meal, and worked on a jigsaw puzzle with the kids. Then Molly, who is seven, wanted to play charades. This she did with gusto, throwing her body into every pose, and sometimes, forgetting that she wasn't supposed to speak, she would kind of whisper the sound she was getting at. At one point, desperate, she resolved to spell out the name of a book with her body, lying on the floor, and forming her flexible limbs into letters. She kept at it no matter how long it took. She was irrepressible.

And so God is with us. If we miss one epiphany, God will keep trying, keep hinting broadly, breaking the rules in order to break through to us. We are invited to join the great game, to live fully and fiercely towards our callings, to stand on our toes to catch a glimpse of the divine along the way.

May the new year open us to God's glorious light, shining star-like on our way. May our hopes and dreams and resolutions lead us closer to the wholeness of life that God desires for us. May the new things that God declares find hearing and hope through each one of us.

Praise be to the Holy One! And Happy New Year. Amen.

Epiphany 1   Acts 10:34-43

God Shows No Partiality

Lois Rose

" . . . God shows no partiality, but in every nation anyone who fears him and does what is right is acceptable to him."

Sometimes God has to hit someone over the head with a two by four in order to get their attention. In the story of the early church which is found in the book of Acts, it happened twice. Otherwise we, the church, wouldn't be here now. The first recipient of the head knock was Paul, on the road to Damascus. The second was Peter. This story is so important that it's worth retelling.

It seems there was a certain Roman soldier named Cornelius who was, by all accounts, a good man, prayerful and generous. He was probably a worshipper of Mithras, the sun god of the Romans, very popular with soldiers. One afternoon he had a terrifying vision of an angel, telling him to send for Peter who had something to tell him. Now anyone who had been following this story at all couldn't help but wonder whether or not someone in heaven hadn't gotten their wires crossed, because Peter was the last person most would have thought of for such a conversation with a Roman. You see Peter, who was an extremely powerful speaker and healer, was also somewhat impatient and intolerant. As far as he was concerned, this new religion was a branch of Judaism, and meant for Jews. He had no patience with non-Jews unless they were willing to adopt all the Jewish customs and rules first. Peter was not alone in this exclusionary attitude, but he was considered the leader of the group that held strongly to this belief.

The next day, as the messengers from Cornelius were on their way to the town in which Peter was staying, Peter was praying earnestly on the roof. It was about noon, very hot, no doubt, and he was hungry. He fell into a trance and saw descending toward him, a large cloth bundle, and in it were all the animals that Jews were not supposed to eat. With it a voice said, "What God has made clean, you must not call unclean." Just in case Peter didn't get it the first time, it happened twice more.

Just then the messengers from Cornelius arrived and took him home with them. Peter was now in the company of non-Jews, maybe even eating with them, something his strict orthodox beliefs did not allow. At their request, he told them about Jesus. He thought at this point that his vision meant that he could tell them the story of Jesus, give them the opportunity for faith. But he had no intention of baptizing them, of initiating them into the fellowship of Christians. They could repent and receive forgiveness, and even believe, but that was as far as it could go. Without baptism they would be a kind of outer circle of believers, acknowledging the truth from the outside.

You must understand that this was going quite far for Peter. Yes, Peter's envelope was being pushed. He had reached the point of graciousness, but not yet of true vision.

But God had other ideas. Before Peter could finish speaking, the Holy Spirit came upon these non-Jews, and they began to speak in tongues and exhibit other signs of the gift. Up until this moment the visitation of the Holy Spirit—which for Peter and his friends was a specific experience that conferred certain wonderful powers on those so endowed—had been reserved for women and men who had been together at the moment the Holy Spirit arrived on the day of Pentecost and a few others who had shown special receptivity. But certainly not for non-Jews.

Yet, there it was. God's profligate powers being bestowed willy nilly on all and sundry, even on unbaptized pagans. What could God be thinking of?

Well, Peter felt he had no choice but to baptize them, which meant they were part of the body of Christ, the organization. And it called into question not only who could be a Christian, but just who could be in that inner circle of apostles. Everything now was up for grabs. How can you run an organization that way?

Peter is working his way through three separate things here, which he is in constant danger of confusing, just as the church has done and just as we do. The first is **faith**. Peter, after his vision asserts that this is open to anyone even non-Jews. God is the God of all, the divine element in all faiths; and people of all faiths can recognize the validity of Jesus' teachings and believe in the power of repentance, of being sorry, of turning away from those acts that divide and destroy. Anyone can hear and believe. For this, Peter says, God shows no partiality.

The second is **order**, the humanly created customs, rules and responsibilities that are meant to contain that faith and of which the ceremony of water baptism is a part. It is the initiation ritual that brings a believer formally into the Christian fellowship. It is an act of will, it is public, and it is a recognition of participation in an organization. It symbolically refers to repentance and belief, but it does not confer those things. For Peter and the other Jerusalem Christians this should be only for Jews and Jewish converts. For the followers of Paul, this became open to all who wished to identify as followers of Christ.

But there is a third element—**the gift of the Holy Spirit**, the experience of being seized by something outside of will or desire and being irrevocably changed. In this experience one is chosen by God or Holiness and it transcends and often contradicts the customs or rules of the institutional church. The action of the Spirit is creative. It changes things. It shakes up the institution. Institutions tend to be exclusive, the Holy Spirit tends to be inclusive. And it can't be predicted. Jesus said, "The wind blows where it chooses, and you hear the sound of it, but you do not know where it comes from or where it goes. So it is with everyone who is born of the Spirit." (John 3:8)

The fledging church had assumed that the experience of the Spirit was a criterium for leadership in the institution. It had assumed two levels of membership, water baptism and baptism in the Spirit. In this instance with Peter, the Spirit behaved in an unexpected manner. Because it tends to do the unexpected, the institutional church has often not known what to do with it. Today, some evangelical churches make it a prerequisite for full membership. Others, like the liberal churches, have variously discouraged the Spirit or confused it with a warm fuzzy sense of community that allows for no overt disagreement.

Peter asks a question at the end of this story which the church has never really answered satisfactorily. "If God gave them the same gift that he gave us when we believed, who was I that could hinder God?"

I would like to suggest three places where the present working of the Spirit is not following expectations.

The fastest growing branch of Christianity right now is Pentecostalism. It makes us nervous because many of the adherents and leaders are uneducated people in third world countries. How can we be sure that their theology is correct? How can we be sure that their rituals are properly performed. But who are we to hinder God?

The most explosive issue in the church right now is the leadership of women. How can the church regulate the theology and rituals of people who don't always show proper respect for tradition? And who are we to hinder God?

The most challenging question facing the church right now is how to communicate effectively with people of other faith traditions. Some would assert that the outcome of this conversation could effect the future of the planet as we attempt to address the problems of large scale war and environmental degradation. The places where they come together most fruitfully are among those branches of each faith where spiritual experience is the focus. These groups are often at the edge of the institutions. Can we not recognize the action of the Holy Spirit in holy women and men of all faiths? "For if God has given them the same gift that was given us when we believed, who are we to hinder God?"

Come, Holy Spirit, come! Amen

Epiphany 2   Psalm 40:1-11
                                            Isaiah 49:1-7

Being God's Song

Carole Ann Camp

There is a Russian folk song that goes:

> If the people lived their lives as if it were a song, for sing-
> ing out of light; provides the music for the stars to be danc-
> ing circles in the night.[3]

So how does one go about "living one's life as if it were
a song?" How are you living your life as if it were a song?

My first response was to think of a song as a dance. What
kind of dance are you?

Are you a minuet? Very formal, following intricate rules?
Following a script? Playing a role? Repeating old established
patterns? Doing precisely what is expected of you? Knowing
that if you deviate only slightly from the pattern, the dance will
be thrown into chaos for everyone? Are you part of the dance,
but in a somewhat detached way; your body going through the
steps, but your mind elsewhere?

Are you a circle dance? Circling around some imaginary
center that occasionally pulls you toward it? Still following the
intricate patterns, but being able to look deep into the eyes of
every other dancer? Holding hands, no beginning and no end?

Are you a couple dance? Flowing and gliding around the
floor in step with only one other? Expertly avoiding collisions
with other couples. Aware of their existence, but independent of

them. Free to make your own patterns as simple or as intricate as you feel at the moment? Are you the leader, or are you the follower? Do you ever change roles? Have you ever thought about changing roles?

Are you dancing alone, but with hundreds of others, keeping time to the beat of the music, but doing your own thing? Pulsating and gyrating to the steady and persistent beat of the drum? Eyes avoiding eyes.

For me personally, being the new song means being the new dance.

But one doesn't have to dance in order to be God's new song. Another way to hear what this means, may have something to do with being in tune.

There is a curious thing about being in tune. All eighty-eight keys on my piano are in tune with each other. But they are all out of tune with other instruments. Everyone who comes to my house has to tune their instruments to my piano. Pianos are very difficult to tune.

In some ways congregations are like that. A single congregation may be in tune with itself but be out of tune with everyone else. And we all know how very difficult it is to retune a whole congregation.

To be in tune. To be attuned to. Does it matter if my piano is only in tune with itself?

I think it is very important to be in tune with oneself. I think it is very important to sing your own song and to dance your own dance. But there is a conundrum here. Certainly most of western psychology advocates for finding one's own tune, finding one's own song, finding one's own drummer. But is that enough? Is that all there is to it?

Is there a universal song? A universal tune? A universal dance to which we might also want to tune ourselves? Is being God's new song different than being a minuet or a polka?

In Psalm 40 the new song that has been put into the mouth, is a song of praise, a song of thanksgiving. Do you live your life as if it were a song of praise? Do you live your life as if it were a song of thanksgiving and gratitude? The psalmist was pulled out of the pit, out of the muck and mire. When one has been plucked out of the pit, it is easy to remember to give thanks to God for deliverance. But what about while one is in the muck and mire, do we still live thanks? Can our song still be one of praise? Can we still dance the dance of gratitude?

At the time of the writing of Isaiah 49, the people were in exile, a difficult time to be giving thanks to God. In Psalm 137 the people wail,

> By the rivers of Babylon—there we sat down and there we wept when we remembered Zion. On the willows there we hung up our harps. For there our captors asked us for songs, and our tormentors asked for mirth, saying, "Sing us one of the songs of Zion!" How could we sing the Lord's song in a foreign land?

For those of us who claim to be followers of the Prince of Peace and the God of Love and Forgiveness, we are in exile. We are in exile in the land of violence. We sit down by the polluted rivers and we weep. We weep knowing of the violence done to our home, the planet earth. We weep with the trees of the rainforest that are being cut down or burned needlessly. We weep for the senseless slaughter of animals. We weep for the children who only know violence as a way of life. We weep for the unemployed and the underemployed. How can we sing the Lord's song in this foreign land?

But isn't that precisely when we should sing God's song? Isn't that precisely when we should **be** God's song?

Throughout the stories in the Bible, we are given clues about how to live our life as if it were a song. In the lesson from Isaiah, we hear that our song is to be a prophetic one, to call the people to a life of peace and justice, hope and joy. We are called to live the song of truth, and to live it so clearly that no one will mistake it for something else. We are called to spread the light. We are called to sing out of the light; the light we know in the life of Jesus. Jesus is a good example of someone who was in tune.

To be God's song means being in tune with God, it means being in tune with oneself, it means being in tune with God's other children, and it means being in tune with the whole of creation including the birds of the air, the fish of the sea, the winds that blow from the four corners of the earth, and the rocks under our feet.

Have you ever listened for the tune a rock is singing? Or the song the trees sing? How close is your song with theirs?

In order for God's wholeness and holiness to be spread to all the nations, those of us who feel as if we are in exile, need to find our song and tune it to God's song.

> If the people lived their lives as if it were a song, for sing-
> ing out of light; provides the music for the stars to be danc-
> ing circles in the night.

Epiphany 3   Psalm 27

On Recovery[4]

Valerie E. Russell

Certain moments in life are marked by traumatic and cataclysmic events when we face the reality of life beyond our control. For those of us who like to believe we are strong and independent, this is devastating.

One week before Christmas when I had a stroke, I came face to face with human and physical limitation. Ever since then, over the last three months, I have been trying to come to terms with those limitations.

My left leg and left arm shut down. They never lost their feeling, they just wouldn't work! The slow process of healing has forced me to adjust my understanding of time. As one of my fellow rehab patients said to me in the heart of the rehabilitation process, "It's hard to be a fast person in a slow body."

"Rehabilitation" is in some ways a misleading term when it comes to strokes. One's effort, exercise, and the difficult work to restore muscle function does help. However, the cells of the brain must find alternative cells to the old ones to create the ability to function in new ways. Again, one must rely on the natural healing process beyond one's control.

In this process, one learns a lot about patience, feelings of abandonment and Grace. Faith becomes the glue which cements together a wall of hope to defend against total despair.

Tears become the body's natural conduit for ameliorating fear and panic. I am told that there is a word for it—"lability",

51

which means a diminished ability to repress tears. I have cried the tears of a lifetime.

Underneath the process of waiting for healing and waiting for doctors and nurses to respond to a signal light, lies the fear of abandonment, and a diminished sense of specialness. The myth of invulnerability and specialness dries up quickly. One does not live by myth but by vulnerability.

I learned again of grace. While there's lots of feeling that the glass is half empty, there's also enormous evidence that the glass is also half full.

The daily stories of the indomitability of the human spirit, the daily acts of courage of people who could easily give up around me, who could have given in to fear and resignation, but who do not, were awesome.

The blessings, prayers and good wishes from friends and members of the church which transforms the crowd into a community, all give one a sense of overwhelming grace. True grace happens in the toughest moments when hope is all one has to cling to.

The institutional church is also caught right now in a kind of stroke-like vulnerability. Many professional academics are proclaiming the patient dead, and arguing that the institutional church and denominations are moribund.

Old institutional norms, and patterns of behavior no longer work. Leaders are forced to examine their old propositions and behavior—to rid themselves of racism, sexism and a variety of other isms which no longer are acceptable as we move into the twenty-first century.

But just as in the case of the stroke victim, there are very different results if the victims of such cataclysmic change are left for dead, or seen as permanently dysfunctional. It's a matter of learning "a new walk and a new talk" . . . of growing new metaphorical brain cells.

When trying to cure social dysfunction and years of oppressive behavior, one must find and practice forgiveness and mercy on the social level which will overcome guilt and paralysis of awareness.

Illness has lessons to teach us which can redirect our personal lives. Social illness can do the same if we can accept it and move forward with open faith toward the future. Mostly, we need to start on the path to new life, since instant Lazarus experiences do not happen very often. So we live our way into a new wholeness, even with the most subtle emerging of a new strength. There is a paradox of grace. It's tough stuff needed for tough times. It is both tough and tender at the same time.

We need to reclaim the "wounded healer" vocation as very real functional definition of who we are trying to be rather than as interesting cute description of who we might be.

When one becomes paralyzed or has dysfunction predominant in their lives, either individually or corporately, grief becomes quite real—one grieves for the life you had when you felt more in control, "on top of things."

Physical illness is safer in expressing such grief than is social dysfunction grief. People sympathize and empathize with the loss of an arm. They don't easily do so when someone finds a vision, hope or dream turned to dust. To feel grief is to claim healing endorphins. It is not to give in to helplessness which leaves one feeling totally victim. Victimization robs the spirit of ego strength and self love. To "give in" to fear is one giant step in the opposite direction of healing.

Grieving, however, while it can be cleansing for the griever can be hard on the griever's support system. It is difficult to know how to receive others' tears and how to be both helpful but encouraging of the expression of one's sadness, panic and reality. Luckily, I had some friends who understood this well.

Having their constant support allowed me to be vulnerable and kept my grief from moving merely into rage. In both individuals and institutions, "victims" retreat into rage because the system does not respond well to vulnerability. We thus create situations where only anger is legitimized as a response to illness and society's dysfunctions. We must find a legitimacy and liturgy for grief. It is one of the keys to the recovery of the vision for healing.

Living in the aftermath of a stroke, or social change, is traumatic. Colleagues and friends must accept and mid-wife the healing at your pace not theirs. This is difficult again as those around you are deeply affected by your recovery pace. Your vulnerability and struggle reminds others of their own and they suffer the slowness of healing as you do. In a world of instant success, this is most difficult. Thus, recovery is not a leap frog movement but a journey of a single step at a time. It is a slow motion version of the resurrection . . . not out of the tomb in a day, or even in three, but a "trek" of the rest of the days of one's life.

Are there lessons that can be learned for the church and institutional behavior from my personal experience of a stroke? I feel there are many. A few are:

1. "Waiting patiently for God" is more than a verse in scripture, but is a fervent dynamic of faith. One must believe unalterably that the Spirit is resident in the healing.

2. All of us are vulnerable beyond our control unless hope, vision (if only dimly) and the community of faith remind and assure us continually that the healing process is like the "spirit groaning in travail" and with us as we wait for the new creation in process.

3. Trust in care-givers and those who challenge you to move beyond your "perceived limits" is crucial. The institutional church needs to groom and employ people who act not only as advocates for change, but those who are "caretakers" who "take care" with the people learning to walk in new ways, who will provide encouragement and an arm to lean on. This is to practice a theology of "accompaniment."

4. Those who carry that trust and who encourage you beyond your perceived limits are the only way one can often dare move ahead into new territory when feeling vulnerable.

5. The Christian community is most powerful when people move beyond their political relations to being most human with each other.

6. Learning to renew functioning after a period of paralysis and dysfunction takes time, but is part of a natural process.

7. Bernie Siegel in *Peace, Love and Healing* says "that creator has given us five senses to help us survive threats from the external world, and a sixth sense, our healing system."[5]
   We need institutionally, as well as individually, to "mobilize" our healing systems. To work on our re-envisioning of

a just world, even as we struggle to mobilize healing for our damaged bodies.

Such effort takes enormous faith and self love right at the moments we do not feel so lovable. With the struggle with physical limitations comes deep anger and frustration with the body and what it cannot do, things once so taken for granted. Yet one must learn to be gentle with the bodily limitations or you will get stuck in self hatred.

Epiphany 4   Micah 6:6-8
                                                Matthew 1:1-12

How Blest Are Those
Who Know Their Need Of God
Shirlee Bromley

A Baptist pastor in Memphis, Tennessee, tells of a time when she and a friend were traveling in the back roads and mountains of North Carolina and decided to stop at a bed-and-breakfast inn. After they checked in and settled into their room, they decided to take a look around the inn. They walked into a small living room "filled with antique furniture and a crazy patchwork quilt on the wall", and there they saw Lily. It didn't take them long to realize that Lily was mentally ill. With a coffee mug in one hand and a cigarette in the other, she began telling them about her thirteen dogs. Her story had no beginning and no ending. She stopped talking as abruptly as she had started.

The next morning they learned that Lily had been living with a guardian in the Midwest. But the guardian was nearing eighty years old and could no longer care for her. So now Lily was staying with her stepbrother, Ron, the forty-five year old owner of the inn. Ron said he was the only one left to care for her. Nancy said to Ron, "You are very generous to open your home to Lily." Ron replied, "Oh, no, it doesn't have anything to do with being generous. I just don't want to see her mistreated."[6]

Jesus tells us that the meek are getting ready to inherit the earth. Jesus identifies the ones who are already receiving God's blessing. The favored of God are those who are the unfavorable ones; the mourners, the meek, the poor in spirit, the oppressed, and the persecuted.

When we start looking for signs of folks being the church, the beatitudes give us some clues for where to look. It's not in our church programs, it's not in our good deeds, our balancing the budget, our goals, our numbers, or how we are managing it all. The beatitudes tell us to look between the cracks; to look in the places where life is falling apart.

Blessed is sometimes translated "happy" or even congratulations. I like the Greek translation "fortunate" or even in our everyday vernacular "lucky are you"—lucky are you if you are in touch with the poor in spirit, the meek, the afflicted, the oppressed, the little ones of this world; fortunate are you if you have noticed who the hurting people are; lucky are you if you know your need of God.

A Hebrew word for the forgotten and oppressed in our society is *anawim*. *Anawim* are the people in the world who are put down by others. Let me name just a few of the people who are put down in our world: women, homosexuals, Jews, Native Americans, Blacks, and we could go on. Why are they put down? Matthew Fox, Creation Spirituality theologian, says that the reason given by the oppressors is that, in some way, these people are or do something against nature.

A missionary in Brazil tells the story of a bounty hunter in the Amazon who was paid to kill Indians. The hunter said that he once shot an Indian who did not die at once but appeared to be in pain and suffering, "just as if he were a human being."

I won't attempt to speak much about the ban on gays in the military today—I know what a volatile subject that is—but I believe that gays, lesbians, bisexuals, transgenderists, all those who have suffered in our society because their sexual orientation is not considered the "norm" are numbered among the *anawim* of our world. And, we who call ourselves the church need to pay attention!

In the United Church of Christ there are one hundred and forty-three churches in our entire denomination who are considered "open and affirming" churches. This means that heterosexuals as well as those of sexual orientations other than heterosexual are invited, welcomed, and affirmed in the church. Fourteen of these churches are here in Massachusetts. There are four hundred and thirty-nine U.C.C. churches in Massachusetts.

As I speak, I'm going to take the liberty from time to time to use the word "gay" generically, referring to those of sexual orientation other than heterosexual. This is not correct and I apologize and struggle with how to use the language to be inclusive of all people. Maybe we can begin to see more clearly how our social situations are constantly evolving and all the many layers of meaning are present and it is no small task to try to sort it all out. One of the things that the media is doing now in relationship to the ban on the gays in the military is interchanging the word gay with sexual preference. This is inaccurate and very uninformed. Our sexual orientation, whatever it is, is God given and to say that it is preference is like saying: I prefer to be left-handed or right-handed; I prefer to be male rather than female; or female rather than male. It is not that simple.

A few years ago in Bangor, Maine, a young teenage boy was tossed off a bridge and killed because he was gay. That's only one case among many of such blatant violence against homosexuals. It would be my guess that nearly every family has a gay person; maybe a son, a daughter, sister, brother, nephew, niece, cousin, uncle, aunt, mother, father. Gays have lived for years in silence and invisibility. The denial and the pain has been colossal. Many gays have turned to alcohol; many have taken their lives. The church has turned them away; turned its back on them. The church says, "You can come but never mention who you are." The church has essentially turned away a vital part of the Body of Christ, and I believe it has not gone unnoticed by God.

Several years ago I attended a conference held in Connecticut where parents of gays spoke out. They now have a national organization called PFLAG, Parents, Families, and Friends of Lesbians and Gays. I was incredibly moved by these parents who have embraced their children and have gone to bat for them. They expressed how much their gay son or daughter has helped them and how they now know more of God because of their gay children.

Can you imagine having a gay son or lesbian daughter and having your friends or people around you say that they are an abomination unto God and don't deserve to live?

The church is called to be embracing to all people. We need to educate ourselves and begin to look at our own contradictions and to see between the cracks.

Many gays and lesbians have fought back. The gay community now has a denomination, the Metropolitan Community Church, which was formed because of their being denied access to churches. Recently, the MCC tried to become a part of the National Council of Churches, asking only for observer status; and they were denied on the grounds that the National Council of Churches must preserve its unity. The National Council of Churches' history is built upon prophetic confrontation of social prejudices. Their refusal to recognize the MCC is a very serious step. [7]

AIDS has been foolishly labeled a "gay" disease by many in the heterosexual population. That's a very perilous mistake as the disease advances across all lines regardless of race, creed, or sex.

Jesus never condemned homosexuals; Jesus did condemn hypocrites, and liars; and he warned against hurting the *anawim*, the little ones.

Matthew Fox tells about the privilege that he had one summer teaching with Sister Jose Hobday, a Franciscan sister and a Native American. One day she took him aside with great seriousness and said that she had a question to put to him as a representative of white society. She said, "I cannot understand the hang-up in white culture and church towards the homosexual. In our native traditions we don't even have a word for 'homosexual.'" Hobday went on to say that it is well known among the Native Americans that often the homosexual was the most spiritual member of the tribe. It was not unusual for the homosexual to be a counselor and mentor to some of the most important chiefs. [8]

Fox said that what Sister Jose was experiencing as an outsider was homophobia. If we lived in a society or a church that was not homophobic, we would not need to speak of it today. Homophobia is the fear of our own homosexual feelings. Society's homophobia is a paranoia that is acted out by trying to blot out the gay community. Many assume that heterosexuality is a biological norm, and that, unless interfered with, all individuals are heterosexual. In the last hundred years questions were raised such as "What causes this deviation from the norm?" "Where did he or she go wrong?" This course of study left only one possibility open to society, to do everything in its power to prevent this deviation. When this failed, a cure was sought for its victims, or a punishment, or a way to drive them underground, preventing any homosexual expression. After all the research, we still do not know why anyone is homosexual or heterosexual. What we know is that we are an infinite variety; what we do know is that we are all unique human persons.

Some of the people of deepest faith that I know are homosexual persons. If we believe that we are created in God's likeness and image, and that it is good that we celebrate our creation and give thanks to our Creator, how can we deny this to others? All people have the right to celebrate who God has created them to be.

In the eighth century BC, the temple in Israel became a monopoly. It became a place of power and control. When an institution controls who has access and who does not, that institution is in trouble. The ancient laws of purity were forms of social control that let some people in and kept other people out. The prophets of old began their critique of what was going on.

Micah, in words that we know well, really sums up the teachings of the prophets Amos, Hosea and Isaiah. Micah says, "This is what God asks of you, only this, to act justly, to love tenderly, and to walk humbly with your God."

We need this same critique in our churches today. We cannot be called the redeemed by Jesus of Nazareth and continue to hate the children of God who may be different from us.

Do you know your need of God? When we know our need of God then I believe we will stop hurting others because we will realize how blessed we are to be loved by God in our uniqueness. We will have no need to bring down another person; we will desire to affirm one another, for this is what the household of God is about, this is what peacemaking is about.

I always feel very humbled by the realization that somehow God loves me. I don't understand it. I only know it's true. And, God loves you, my friends, just as you are. Do you know it?

Do you know your need of God? If you do, you are most lucky! God Bless you. Amen

Epiphany 5   1 Corinthians 2:1-16

Will I Get To See God?

Betsy Waters

It was Sunday. Grandma was helping her grandchild with the final preparations for church.

"Grandma?" One of those unexpected childhood conversations began. "Will I get to see God at church?"

She paused, unsure of what to say next. "I don't think so, dear. God's off in heaven with grandpa."

The conversation went elsewhere, as such conversations tend to do, but soon after the pair arrived at church, it resumed again.

"Grandma, Grandma, we do get to see God in church." The child pointed with great excitement to the pastor dressed in her robe and embroidered vestments. "There she is!"

There are many ways to recognize God. We find God in prayers to Jesus, in our faith that our departed loved ones are cared for, in the Bible stories we study and the people who teach us these stories, in the friends and family whom we love and who love us, and in the magic, mysterious, precious moments of life. I hope we find God in church, but I also trust that we recognize God's presence in the work place, in schools, in our homes, and in nature. Spirit is alive in our midst, we need only open our ears and eyes.

But talking about God, sharing our experiences, especially the ones that are nearest and most precious, that's not always easy. Even Paul acknowledges the difficulty of such intimate sharing. Paul confesses to his congregation that talking about God makes him tremble. He shakes in his boots when he imagines telling about his relationship with the Holy. Paul lets us know that he worries about what he'll say. Will he choose the right words, the right image? He might stammer as he talks or not show the preciousness of his vision or in some way not convey the sacredness which God has revealed in his life. Paul was afraid he was somehow not good enough to speak of his hidden, personal relationship with the Holy.

We know from other passages that Paul did not know Jesus personally. Paul had not come to believe through the stories about Jesus or his teachings. No, Paul's faith was based on one or more mystical experiences. Paul's mystical experience, his vision on the road to Damascus, turned his whole life upside down. Until then, Paul had been a Jewish Pharisee who had persecuted those who believed in Jesus. It is likely that he traveled from village to village ferreting out those who professed Jesus Christ as Lord and attacked them publicly, calling them names or worse.

But then on the road to Damascus he was, to use his own words, "seized by Jesus the Lord." Blinded by the Light. The world, as he had known it, stopped. Everything about Paul was reordered. His beliefs shifted, his job was redefined. His life's purpose changed. All the elements of his life were shaken up and all he could hold onto was this mystical experience where the Christ crucified on the cross was revealed to him.

Paul writes a letter to the congregation in Corinth telling them that he comes to them knowing nothing except Christ and Christ's death on the cross. Paul was a very well educated man. He had received both Greek education and the training of a

Jewish Pharisee. Most likely he knew philosophy, writing and mathematics; and he knew the Hebrew scriptures, frontwards and backwards. Yet now, all of Paul's education became secondary to his relationship with God through Christ. The power of that event was so significant that Paul not only changed his own life, he became willing, despite fear and trembling, to proclaim his relationship with Jesus, dead on the cross and then raised. Paul knew Christ was resurrected. He had experienced the resurrected Christ for himself, personally in his mystical encounter. In that blinding vision, Paul recognized that Jesus who was crucified was the Christ, the beginning of the new Creation. No religious authority—be it Jew or Greek—could convince him otherwise!

Believing in Christ crucified was more radical than perhaps we can immediately understand. What Paul professed conflicted with prevailing thought. To Jews of Paul's day, worshipping a dead man's body would not only seem silly, it would have been offensive. Jewish religious practices made dead bodies unclean—off limits. Jews were hands-off when it came to dead people. In the cult of Judaism, touching dead bodies meant that a person had to be separated from the community for a day or more. Jews would find the idea of worshipping a dead Jesus almost gross. And yet Paul, a Jew, found that his experience was so profound and filled with truth, that he turned away from traditional practices. He was so convinced that his spiritual encounter with the Christ was real that he risked insult and rejections to proclaim what had been revealed to him.

But it wasn't just Jews who would reject a Christ crucified. To the Greeks, worshipping a man who had been crucified would make no sense either. Greeks knew that political authorities would execute by crucifixion only the most disgusting criminal for committing the most heinous crimes. Other people might be executed, but in more humane ways. A Greek would assume that anyone who was crucified would have had to be a despicable man, barely worth being called a human being. Worshipping someone who was executed by crucifixion might seem like elevating a Charles Manson to sainthood, a ridiculous thought for any sane individual.

And yet Paul's mystical experience superseded logic and customs. Paul knew directly from his spiritual encounter, that Jesus was the Christ. Paul knew intensely and personally from his experience that Christ had been raised and conquered death. Paul didn't need anyone else to tell him what to believe. He didn't need anyone to believe the same thing he believed in order to tell his story. And yet each of us can appreciate the fear and trembling Paul must have felt to assert his beliefs in the face of prevailing attitudes. Scary stuff.

Proclaiming what we know about God can be scary stuff for us too. Each of us has had experiences of God even though it may be hard to recognize and claim them.

How do you know God? How have you experienced the Holy moving in your life? Recall experiences that are significant to you as you've come to believe. When have you felt spiritual support? Was the Spirit present to you in a time of loneliness, personal suffering, or death? Have you called out in prayer? Have you felt the everlasting arms sustaining you? Have you? Remember.

Have you experienced God through people, people who love you, who accept you as you are, who listen? Remember, see their faces and thank the God who was present where two or three gathered.

Have you recognized God in an encounter with a stranger; someone there when you needed them or someone whose need you responded to? There, with strangers, hearts opened, and each giving and receiving more than ever seemed possible? Remember.

It is such a mystery, such a miracle that God supplies all that is needed and more. We can recognize God's presence in meeting with strangers, in giving and receiving, in smiles, gestures, and gifts.

Have you met God in silence or prayer, in the middle of the night or an ecstatic experience, in making love or forgiving a grievance? Remember the precious moments when God has been made known to you, and let your heart be filled with gratitude.

How might you share the joys and blessings that have bubbled into your life? How might you share your connection with the Holy? Sharing stories is one way we proclaim the good news— the gospel. We can tell the old, Biblical and historic stories of how God moved in people's lives through good times and bad. We can also tell the stories of how Spirit is alive in our midst, quelling doubts and fears, opening joys and blessings.

Yet somehow, we, supposedly mature folk, stumble around trying to identify when we see God. And adults often have more trouble sharing our experiences of God than children do.

Here is another letter sharing a personal experience with God. This letter is not from Paul but from Herbert, quoted from *More Children's Letters To God*.

Dear God, Sometimes I think I can see you. I think I saw you last night. Is that a bad thing to say? I would like to very much. My mommy says you are always very near to us. Your friend, Herbert[9]

Herbert, I think you can see God. I think each of us has many opportunities to see God. I'm glad you caught a glimpse and wrote to tell about it. Just like you, we long to see God very much. And just like you and Saint Paul we worry about what we will say and how it might get received. Herbert, I thank you for sharing what you have experienced with us. Each of us will be richer for it. And hopefully, we will learn and share our experiences of Spirit with each other. Hopefully, we, too, can spread the good news of God with us.

Epiphany 6

Deuteronomy 30:15-20
1 Corinthians 3:1-9
Matthew 5:21-37

Of Towels And Tradition

Susan L. Boone

How do you fold your towels? I know that seems like a trivial question, but it can be pretty important in our house. I happen to fold them in thirds, in thirds the long way and then in thirds again. I live with someone, however, who folds towels in quarters, and although I do not check out linen closets, I know of people who fold them in half and then roll them up.

Now I fold my towels in thirds because that's how my mother did it. No doubt she folded them in thirds because her mother did it that way. I have no idea why my grandmother might have folded her towels in thirds, although it may have been because they fit better in her linen closet or it may have been how her mother did it. I suspect the person I live with folds the towels in quarters because that's the way his mother did it. I mean it's tradition, what may seem like a trivial one, but one that is handed down through the generations. Ah, traditions! It's tough to mess with them.

I like to think that I am pretty broad-minded about this issue, but when I look in my linen closet and see towels folded in quarters there among the ones that I have neatly folded in thirds, it makes me uncomfortable. Ah tradition! Now there are a number of ways this dilemma can be solved. First of all, I can take over the laundry completely, not let anyone else do it so that I can maintain control over my linen closet and my tradition; but that's no fun and lots of work, and besides laundry is not my most favorite thing to do. Also it might be denying another of their right to their family towel folding tradition. I could let my partner take over the laundry, and the linen closet and have all the towels folded in quarters, but that's unlikely. I could loosen up a bit (heaven forbid) and not be so anxious about those other folded towels in the linen closet, or we could throw tradition completely out of the window and just use the towels from the laundry basket and not fold them at all (which has happened on more occasions than I care to remember).

This household tradition is minor compared to the one about who's mother's Thanksgiving turkey dressing is traditional, or the tradition of the dreadful store bought fruitcakes that float around at Christmas, or which pew one sits in on Sunday morning. It takes a stout heart to rock the boat and challenge a tradition, even if the tradition has no meaning for us any more.

Now most of these can be resolved with some sense of humor and a little bit of courage, but breaking other traditions is more costly. Think of what happened the last time you challenged a long held tradition in your family. Think of what happened the last time we asked people to change their seats on Sunday morning. What happens when a tradition that has begun life on the scale of the linen closet ends up as something sacred and holy?

There are many that move on up the ladder of importance. Ones that cause church fights. One might ask, for example, about the origin of traditions such as why we cover the communion bread with white napkins. Why not blue or green? Why at all? What is the purpose of the altar rail? Why do people stand up to sing hymns or when the money comes down the aisle, but sit for prayer?

Another is an even bigger one, one that not only causes church fights, but is something that church revolutions are made of: the issue of the ordination of women, gays and lesbians. If any of you followed the turmoil in the church of England as a result of the ordination of women you know what I mean. In the text from Corinthians, Paul is dealing with just such an issue, the issue of leadership in the church at Corinth. There is jealously and quarreling over who belongs to whom, and who the leaders are.

I am not about to totally debunk tradition, because I believe that we all need some kind of steadiness and consistency in our lives, something we can count on, something that honors our paths and our history. But the tension between our need for constancy and our need to move on is a tough balancing act. Also, sometimes sacred tradition is based on things not very sacred at all and not very equitable or fair either. Sometimes tradition immobilizes us and prevents us from moving forward, from looking at things differently, from recognizing the gifts that people have to offer.

In the text from Matthew, Jesus is questioning the ancient Old Testament laws. It's curious that the Old Testament readings for this morning tell us that the only way to find God is by following the rules. But in Matthew, Jesus is telling us to rethink the old rules, the old traditions. He says, "You have heard that it was said to those of ancient times, but I say to you . . . " The rules were ancient ones which had become law over time. Often times we find that the traditions that are intended to help us are in fact keeping us from moving on, holding us back. As we know, Jesus was a master at breaking rules, he was always challenging the status quo.

Whenever anyone challenges tradition and the status quo, and I think every generation does this to a certain extent, it upsets the holders of that tradition, and people get angry and upset. Words like heresy and nonbeliever start surfacing. We look in our linen closets and see the towels folded wrong and think that the world is going to hell in a handbasket. Over the centuries traditions have been challenged in major ways. Jesus got into all kinds of trouble. He challenged the old laws and the world has not been the same since. In 1517 Martin Luther also got into deep trouble by nailing his ninety-five theses to the Wittenberg Castle church door, and Christianity has never been the same since. In the wider church today there is another reformation struggling to be born: a new questioning of tradition, a new quest to find meaning in that tradition, a new examination of the origins of traditions we have held for centuries, new challenges from previously unheard voices that are asking questions. Are they fair? Are they justice-making? Are they peace keeping? Do they free people or contribute to their oppression? Do they lift us up or hold us down?

Interestingly enough the folks in Jesus' time and in Luther's time probably had no idea that they were living in such a momentous era. Making sure their families were fed, their children taken care of, and their towels folded correctly, were probably all they had time to worry about.

Celebration is one of the best kinds of traditions and Jesus himself obviously loved a celebration. He used them as the basis for many of his stories and parables, and despite his challenges to the Jewish law, he was a Jew and tradition was very much a part of his culture.

One of his greatest traditions was having a meal with his friends. The early Christian community told and retold this story, reenacted it over and over and its meaning took root in their lives. As we break bread together today, let us do two things. Let us honor that tradition of sharing the bread and the cup together and the fellowship we hold with one another, but let us also honor Jesus' revolutionary challenge to live with courage, to make peace, to break those rules that enslave us, and to shake up the world with love.

So be it

Epiphany 7   Matthew 5:38-48

Love Our Enemies? You Gotta Be Kidding!

Shirlee Bromley

In the sermon on the Mount Jesus gives the disciples an ear full. Throughout the sermon, Jesus says "you have heard it said, but I say unto you . . . be reconciled to your neighbor . . . do not look lustfully at another . . . do not commit adultery in your heart . . . do not swear oaths . . . let your yes mean yes and your no mean no!" Jesus continues, "You have heard it said, 'you shall love your neighbor and hate your enemy,' but I say to you, Love your enemies and pray for those who persecute you." And then Jesus wraps it all up, "Be perfect, as God is perfect!" Whew!

Can't you imagine the disciples about this time? "Jesus, how can we possibly do all that? And, love our enemies, too, you gotta be kidding! You gotta be kidding!" How can we love our enemies? Who are our enemies?

There is a poignant story about a German couple by the name of Hildegard and Jean Goss-Mayr who met with a group of Polish Christians in Warsaw ten years after the end of World War II. At one point during the meeting they asked this Polish group if they would be willing to meet with Christians from West Germany? They expressed that they wanted to ask forgiveness for what Germany did to Poland during the war and to begin to build a new relationship. At first there was silence on the part of the Polish people. Then someone spoke up vehemently and said: "Hildegard, we love you, you are our friends,

75

but what you are asking is impossible. Each stone of Warsaw is soaked in Polish blood! We cannot forgive!" Even after ten years the war wounds were just too deep.

Before the group parted for the evening, the Goss-Mayrs suggested that they say the Lord's Prayer together. All joined in willingly. But at the point of praying "forgive us our sins as we forgive . . . " the group suddenly halted their prayer. They couldn't speak. But then, out of the silence, the one who had spoken most vehemently said softly, "I must say yes to you. I could not any more pray the Our Father, I could no longer call myself a Christian, if I refuse to forgive. Humanly speaking, I cannot do it; but God will give me the strength!" A year and a half later, the Polish and West German Christians met in Vienna. Friendships made at the meeting continue today[10]

It is pretty clear who the enemy is in this story. We can identify the enemies in war but one must wonder as a nation, now that the cold war is over, if we don't continue to invent enemies because we won't look at our national shadow. But do we know our own enemies? You and me? Our church?

Several years ago I was seeing a therapist in the Boston area. I remember telling my therapist about someone who really bugged me. "What is in that other person that is like you?" What a thing to say! Of course, there wasn't anything in that other person that was like me. I didn't like that very much. Therapists tell us that when there is something in another human being that is able to hook us, it is probably because it is a reflection of our shadow side, a mirror of the part of ourselves that we don't like, that part we have repressed and don't want to accept in ourselves. But it may very well be something that we readily reject in another.

Jesus says, "Why do you see the speck in your neighbor's eye, but do not notice the log in your own eye?"

It's all tied in with this business of being perfect. Perfectionists are perfect only by comparison. Perfectionists must have someone to look down on in order to raise themselves up, thus there is really a secret need for enemies. Scholars tell us that Jesus could not have said, "Be perfect." There was no such word, or even concept, in Aramaic or Hebrew. In this text Matthew has taken a Greek translation of the Hebrew word *tamin* which means "whole, complete, finished, entire, to have integrity." Our being perfect, our wholeness is in process—and always will be in this life—and we can never accomplish this wholeness ourselves, only with God's help and grace.

Jesus said, "How can you say to your neighbor, let me take the speck out of your eye while the log is in your own eye? . . . First take the log out of your own eye, and then you will see clearly to take the speck out of your neighbor's eye."

Walter Wink, Biblical scholar, lecturer and author, says that this passage is the earliest known teaching of projection. Jesus was way ahead of his day. When we encounter people who remind us of things we hate about ourselves and have repressed, we will involuntarily project onto them what has been stirred up in our own unconscious. We are prevented from loving our enemies because we need them as targets for our own projections. That way we don't have to look at our own "stuff." The "splinter" in the other's eye is a chip off the same log that is in one's own eye. We see in the other what we will not see in ourselves. Sometimes we might say, "I may have a few problems, a little splinter perhaps, but that person is really bad—a log!" I grew up in logging country and certainly know that there is big difference between a log and a little splinter. The log in an eye totally blinds; there is room for nothing else. It prevents us from seeing objectively. Removing the log from my own eye enables me to see more clearly how to help my neighbor remove his or her splinter.

Last fall three of us from our church had the privilege of going to a workshop led by Walter and June Wink. Walter did a role play to help us understand what Jesus was really saying in the Sermon on the Mount, and we did exercises that helped us name our own enemies. In Wink's book entitled *Engaging The Powers*, he tells about doing a workshop where a pastor who was present named his enemy as a lay person in the church. Imagine that? The pastor wrote of his enemy, "He wants to be in on every decision, whether he is involved or not." This was one of the characteristics the pastor had checked off on his list that was also true of himself. The "enemy" was a lay leader who insisted that he had to confirm every decision made by any group in the church. The pastor, who saw the same tendency in himself, began to acknowledge that both he and this lay leader had a deep need to control everything.

Can you imagine such a thing? Pastors who want to control? I couldn't possibly identify with that! It's probably the hardest thing for us as pastors to know when to use our authority and when to let go. It's all very threatening for us at times. So much can get triggered within us! Control is, without a doubt, an issue for us all.

Let's hear the dialogue with the pastor.

The pastor was asked, "Why do you need to control everything?"

He said "Because, if things go wrong, I'll get blamed."

"What fear lies behind the need to control everything?"

"The fear that everything will crumble. That I'll be a failure who's not loved."

"Can you think back in your life to times when you felt this way?" The pastor could. "Now, put yourself in your enemy's shoes. What fear drives him to need so much control?"

The pastor responded, "He's a retired farmer who milked five hundred cows a day. That's a big operation. He's sixty-six, and he's just turned the farm over to his son. I think he feels his life is slipping away from him. And here I come trying to force him to release control on the whole church, too! "[11]

It was a very important dynamic for the pastor to discover. Both to see what the lay person was doing and to see the same tendency in himself. Without realizing it they were simply getting locked in an unconscious power struggle. It did not mean that the pastor and everyone else had to give in to the man, but to sense the pain and desperation that he was experiencing will make it easier to love and understand him.

Our enemies bring us a gift. Our enemies are great teachers. Our enemies help us to see aspects of ourselves that we cannot discover any other way than through them. Our friends seldom tell us these things; that's precisely why they are our friends because they overlook and ignore this part of us. We cannot come to terms with our shadow except through our enemies.

The church will be a stronger place when it can name its enemies. Who are the enemies in the church? Are they close at hand? I will leave this question for us to ponder.

There's one more enemy that I'd like to mention. Jesus didn't say this but I believe it's implied. It's a saying we know well, "We are our own worst enemies, I am my own worst enemy." I think it's true, because of the difficulty of loving ourselves and accepting ourselves.

I'm a rather sensitive person. I've always lived more in my feelings than anywhere. I've been told that I'm too sensitive. There's a lot of truth in that. Being sensitive has been my blessing and my curse, but it is so much of who I am; and it is certainly my growing edge in my life and ministry.

For years I carried something in my being that made me sad every time I thought about it. It may sound silly to you, but it wasn't to me.

It was during the war. We were living just outside a small town called Mount Vernon in Washington state. I was five years old. Sometimes we went to the movies as a family on Saturday night. This particular Saturday night there were two pictures showing. My Dad and brother wanted to go to a war film. My Mom wanted to go to a romantic love story movie. I had the freedom to choose, but at five years old I felt torn. I didn't want my mother to go alone, but I didn't want to miss out on what my brothers were seeing either. Reluctantly, I went with my Dad and brothers. I had a miserable time. That night I cried myself to sleep because I felt I had let my mother be all alone. I carried that sad feeling for years, well into my adult life. Finally, not so many years ago, I brought the happening up to my Mom. She could hardly remember it, and then she said to me, "Honey, I was fine, I was glad to be alone for a little while and have some time to myself." I was so relieved. My Mom and I are different inside, what I feel is not what she may feel. We begin projecting at five years old and probably earlier. It was such a relief for me to face what I innocently carried from my early childhood. Can you imagine the ton of stuff we carry with us? What do you carry? It's not too late to check it out. Can you name it, embrace it and move towards it so that it can no longer have a hold on you?

Jesus invites us to love our enemies, pray for them, love the enemy that is even in ourselves, so that we can be free and choose life. This is the way of life. Amen.

Epiphany 8   Matthew 6:24-34

Says Who?

Frances Ruthven

> We are to realize the insignificance of things like food and
> clothing and to remember that there are some things beyond
> our control. We are to overcome the evil of care by filling
> the mind and heart with the concerns of the kingdom of
> God, a great and soul-filling and mind absorbing . . . [12]

The thoughts so bluntly expressed by this Biblical commentator have all too often been echoed in the theologies of those of us who have never known what it means to worry about food or clothing. Yet as I anticipate my first New England winter in almost twelve years, I find it hard, even in my comfortable and warm surroundings, to hear such words when I know that there are those in our country and in our world who must be concerned about what they will eat, or what they will wear. For many, where they will lay their head tonight and the night after that also weighs heavily, and many of those who will be worrying are mothers and their children.

It is hard to believe that Jesus, the Jesus who prayed, "give us this day, our daily bread," could have meant anything like such an interpretation when he spoke the now famous words from the Sermon on the Mount. Yet, there they are, as plain as day:

> Therefore I tell you, do not worry about your life, what you
> will eat or what you will drink, or about your body, what
> you will wear.

The fact that God feeds the birds and clothes the lilies of the field is little consolation to those who are actually without food or clothing. In fact, it can feel like a condemnation. Why would God care more about birds and flowers than about the poor and disenfranchised? Are they not as valuable as flowers and birds? Judging by the political climate expressed in the recent mid-term elections, some in our society are all too ready to answer that question with a resounding NO!

We could simply write off our discomfort with this passage to the fact that the problem is not Jesus, but Matthew. He is always spiritualizing everything. Remember his version of the Beatitudes—"Blessed are the poor in spirit." (5:3)—as opposed to Luke's version "Blessed are the poor." But Luke includes this same passage:

> Therefore, I tell you do not worry about your life, what you
> will eat, or about your body, what you will wear. For life is
> more than food, and the body more than clothing (12:22)

If we cannot write this scripture off, then what can we do with it? What value can we glean from it without condemning those who are without, and have no choice but to worry? How can we affirm that life is truly more than food and the body more than clothing, without dismissing their importance.

The key to understanding this passage lies, I believe, in knowing who said these things, and to whom they are being said. "Jesus is saying these things to his disciples, of course!" you might say. And some have thus interpreted this passage as being an ethic of radical obedience appropriate only for Jesus' closest disciples. But that is not the whole story. Yes, Jesus is saying these things to his disciples, but the author of Matthew is also saying these things to the church of which she/he was a part; and knowing who they were, and the circumstance in which they lived, might give us some insight into our situation and what this passage might mean for us.

The Sermon on the Mount as we have received it in Matthew was written for a first century Jewish Christian community beset by conflict and division. [13]Not only was it being persecuted from without by "official Judaism" as embodied in the scribes and Pharisees; it was also in the midst of a profound internal crisis over how to interpret the teachings of Jesus that had been handed down to it. The church of Matthew was no longer a homogeneous group. Rather it was a mix; and with that mix came varied interpretations of Jesus' ministry, death and resurrection. These various interpretations were vying for authority.

There were those, who because of their faithfulness to Jesus, had had to flee for their lives. They had become itinerant missionaries depending on the hospitality of others for shelter, food, and clothing. At the other end of the spectrum were those, who for fear of persecution and loss of material goods, claimed to be followers of Jesus in private, but in public would not proclaim or live by his teaching.

It was this latter group, with divided loyalties, to whom our passage was directed. Matthew was concerned that the church was being dominated by those who thought they could successfully serve both God and mammon, or wealth. These were not people without means. They were not people who suffered from malnourishment or whose clothes were tattered and torn. Rather they were people like us; people who had enough food in their cupboards and whose closets contained outfits for every occasion. They were not necessarily wealthy, but they were people of means who were unwilling to risk what they had or what they hoped to have for the sake of the Gospel.

Matthew's fellow Christians were not people whose experience of need caused them anxiety about food and clothing. They had never experienced life without the basic necessities of life. Rather, they were people whose greed caused their anxiety and their anxiety was not limited to concern for basic human needs; they were anxious about everything over which they did not have immediate control. What better example is there of that over which we have no control than the future?

The root of the difficulty for the members of Matthew's church was their lack of trust. Not only did they distrust God, they distrusted their own experience. The fact that they had never gone hungry or naked was not enough to engender their trust. They still felt the need to try to control things; to ensure that tomorrow and the next day were already arranged for.

The behavior exhibited by the people in Matthew's congregation was what we now refer to by the catch phrase "addictive." One of the characteristics of addictive behavior is the fear of being without whatever it is one is addicted to. People suffering from addictions think about the next drink, the next hit, the next meal, the next trip to the mall before they have finished feeling the effects of the current high. They believe that they can control situations, especially the addiction; but, in fact, the addiction totally controls them. Their lives are completely oriented toward feeding that appetite. All their time, energy, creativity, emotions, are geared toward making sure the addiction is satisfied.

The most successful treatment program for people with addictions is the twelve-step program. It is no coincidence that the first step on the road to recovery for those with addictions is giving themselves over to a higher power. Matthew's community was made up of individuals, symbolized by the rich young man of Chapter 19, who were addicted to their possessions.

The young man had approached Jesus asking what he must do in order to have eternal life. At first Jesus told him that he must keep the commandments. When the young man asked which ones he must keep, Jesus enumerated the commandments regarding murder, theft, adultery, bearing false witness, and honoring one's father and mother; and he summed up the rest in the commandments to love one's neighbor as one's self. The young man answered that he had kept all of these, and pressed Jesus to tell him what, if anything, he still lacked. Jesus responded that if he wished to be perfect, then he must go home, sell all his possessions, give the proceeds to the poor, and then come and follow Jesus. "When the young man heard this word, he went away grieving, for he had many possessions." (19:22) He could not bear to give up his many possessions. Their hold on him was greater than his desire for eternal life. His only hope of ending that addiction was to give himself over totally and completely to a higher power; to God. He could not continue to try and serve both.

To give oneself over to God means to take each day as it comes; and to deal with the challenges of that day rather than anticipating what might happen tomorrow or the day after that. For the alcoholic it means concentrating on saying no to the drink that you want right now, today. If you can get through today without the drink, then you can deal with tomorrow when it arrives. For those who are obsessed with material goods it means being satisfied with what you need to get through today, and facing tomorrow's needs tomorrow. When those who have are able to concentrate simply on their needs for the day, when they are able to let go of tomorrow, then they are able to practice the justice that serves to empower and enable those who are without. When one can never get enough for oneself, then one is not going to be sharing what one has with others. The hypocrisy practiced by those attempting to serve both God and wealth in the church of Matthew's day was undermining the justice which Matthew believed to be the heart of the Gospel.[14]

Matthew is not telling us in this passage from the Sermon on the Mount that food and clothing are unimportant; or even that they are less important on the hierarchical scale, especially if you don't have either of them. Those things are important and God knows that. This passage is not addressed to those who have to struggle each day just to survive; although the fact that God should be first in everyone's lives, rich and poor alike, is certainly true. Rather this passage is addressed to people who have too much, who want too much, who think they cannot live without more and more and more; and who live in fear of having less. It is addressed to people like me and like you who live in a culture that places a high value on things and possessing things. It is a reminder to us that those who claim to follow Christ, but have given themselves over to other powers, are undermining the Gospel and contributing to the disenfranchisement of our sisters and brothers. It is a reminder that we must make a choice about whom we will serve. And if we, like the rich young man, are filled with grief over the prospect of the impossibility of breaking our addictions, then it is a reminder that what is not possible for human beings is possible with God.

Epiphany 9   Psalm 31:1-5, 19-25
                                               Romans 1:16-17; 3:22-28

God's Circle Of Help

Barbara Kline Seamon

Where do we turn in times of trouble? How do we help those in need? It is the role of the church to extend God's light into the world; to ease, to aid and to lighten the burden we bear.

The Psalmist wrote these encouraging words addressing our Lord: "In you, O Lord, I seek refuge; do not let me ever be put to shame; in your righteousness deliver me."

Epiphany is the season of the church year when we commemorate the coming of God's light to the world. A time in which we celebrate the manifestation of Jesus Christ to the world, a time of wonder and awe. It is also a tranquil time to re-group after Christmas glitter. And to be reminded we owe to each other an obligation not of casual charity, but of gladly-given human help along the way.

The text from Romans speaks of the coming of the light into the world. It describes the vast range of God's light no longer limited by the parameters of the law. It tells of a faith that by it-self makes us just, that reaches beyong the requirements of the law. It tells of a faith that has been, from the beginning, the very foundation of the church.

I have been asked to retell an important family story. It is one in which I learned as a child an important lesson about the church, and how we can be personally involved in extending God's light into the world. It is a story that taught me that one family can make a difference in the life of another and that even one church can help another.

It begins with my home church and my grandmother before I was born. It begins with a couple who lived in the Russian Ukraine.

Ivan and Helen Chernish had no home or community. Their home had been occupied by the Germans during the War and then later by the Russians. They were a young couple, recently married. Ivan was a large man and had been put to hard labor in the work camps. He had deep scars on his back from many beatings. Helen had a baby while in the camp, a baby that was taken from her, never to be seen again. The year was 1949.

My church, The First Methodist Church, sought at that time to help some of the countries overseas that had been devastated by World War II. The church combined its efforts and sent money, supplies, and prayers. They worked hard to find ways of helping people in those countries.

My grandmother, Mabel Fisher, was committed to this effort. Not unlike many of you, she worked long hours in the church sewing and baking to raise money. She worked hard to educate others about Christian service. After long and difficult deliberations the church decided on a mission that would require all its effort and resources.

The church would bring three families to America from the Russian Ukraine. These families would need homes, jobs, and a spiritual community.

My grandparents volunteered their home and Ivan and Helen Chernish came to live with them. The Chernishes spoke no English, so my grandparents found an interpreter. The Chernishes trusted no one, and this made their relationship with

my grandparents difficult. Helen was pregnant and very frightened. She refused to go to the hospital because the only hospitals
she had known had been places of brutality. She had lost one
child already, something my grandmother understood since she
had lost two herself. Fortunately, my grandmother's brothers
were doctors and were able to arrange home care for Helen and
her baby who was premature and very small. My grandmother
was terrified he would not live. For a year Helen, Ivan and the
baby, Johnny, lived with my grandparents. Slowly a warm rap-
port developed. The baby, to everyone's delight, grew large and
strong.

Ivan went to work in a local mill, and Helen cared for her
baby son. Soon the church pooled the resources of 100 families
who donated $100 each. A deposit was made on a house not too
far from the church, and the Chernish family moved into the
first home of their own in this country.

A few years later, in 1954, another baby was born into their
family, a girl named Ann. That was the same year I was born. I
grew up playing with Ann, and one day in particular, I remember well. The sun was bright and warm and we were playing in
my grandmother's back yard. We were playing a game in which
we sang a song that required you to give your full name. I remember going first, "My name is Barbara Lynn Kline." Then
it was Ann's turn. She sang, "My name is Ann Mabel
Chernish." When I heard that I stopped singing. I had never
known anyone but my grandmother to have that funny name
Mabel. But I could tell Ann was not embarrassed. She stood up
straight and said her name proudly . So I asked how she got my
grandmother's name. She replied very seriously, "My mother

gave me your grandmother's name because she gave us our first home. She wants me to remember always."

I was not sure exactly what that meant, but I knew it was very important to Ann. My grandmother was a part of her life, a part of her name.

She had been told to remember. I, too, have remembered.

I grew up remembering; I had learned that you can touch the life of another in an important way. It takes time and effort; it requires sacrifices. And it is the way I first saw the coming of God's light into the whole world.

Even as a child I understood this. It was not theoretical. I had seen Ann's face, and I knew her story. A family that had been foreign to me had become a part of my own. A family that had come from far away, that spoke another language, that I had very little in common with, had become close.

As I consider this story now, I remember these verses in Ephesians 2. "But now in Christ Jesus ye who sometimes were afar off are made nigh by the blood of Christ . . . . Now therefore we are no more stranger and foreigners, but fellow citizens with the saints, and the household of God."

When my grandmother died, I inherited some of her favorite devotional books. In one I found this quote:

> Our spiritual home is the place where our true character is built; where sacrifices to contribute to the happiness of others are made, and where love has taken up its abode.

I think this is a lovely definition of our spiritual home as a church. As a pastor I see much struggling and suffering as people try to survive difficult circumstances alone. Our churches can be places where we build our character. Our churches can be places where we make real sacrifices for one another. Our churches can be places where love flourishes.

My mother told me that one bright fall day, years later, when she was driving past my grandparent's home, she saw Ivan Chernish raking leaves on the front lawn. They had grown too old to do much work themselves. My mother told me that even from her car she could see the scars on Ivan's back. It struck her that now he was helping her parents. The circle of help never ends.

Our God calls us sometimes from a hostile and brutal world into a community where Christ knows our pain and our struggles. Many of us come to our churches with deep emotional scars, deep physical scars; yet our God calls us to a place where no one is a stranger, a place where no law separates us, a place where everyone is willing to give.

This is our church, this is our spiritual home where, as the body of Christ, we can reach out into the whole world with the light of God.

lent

Lent 1   Genesis 2:4, 3:7
                                                  Romans 5:12-21
                                                  Matthew 4:1-11

Gasping For God

Jennifer Phillips

The Holy Spirit drives Jesus into the wilderness where he
fasts for forty days; and, Matthew tells us, after this he was hungry. Indeed. And then the tempter came to him; and afterward,
the ministering angels. We look to Jesus, more earnestly than
ever this season as a model of holiness.

How are we to be holy? Specifically, on this Sunday in
which we have heard once again the story of the calling into being of the creation and us in it, I ask you to consider, how are
we to be holy towards our world? For the holiness of surrender
in prayer, about which many of you heard on Ash Wednesday,
leads forward into the external universe in one unbroken motion.
It is not possible to be transformed in prayer without being transformed in action; the intimate acquaintance with God is of a
piece without relationship with God's creation.

Reading Genesis, I was struck with a deep fellow-feeling for
the foreparents, Adam and Eve and their archetypal desire for
the knowledge of good and evil. And even as a child of the fruit-
eaters, I realize that I and we do not know, like God, the simple
differences of good and evil. We wrestle with ambiguity, we
weigh costs and benefits, ends and means. We suffer and cause
suffering, caught in the middle ground.

In the environment of rich knowledge of the Harvard research establishment, scientists have succeeded in breeding a small white mouse that through genetic engineering will inevitably develop cancers during its lifetime—the oncomouse. For medical scientists, and all of us, this artifact is a great boon. For it allows the testing and development of anticancer drugs, providing a consistent model for gathering experimental knowledge to save human lives. Ethicists have argued over this mouse and declared, for the most part, that the great benefit in preserving human life outweighs the cost to the creature of being born to suffer and die, by human intention. The oncomouse is by no means the only creature we breed to suffer and die for human benefit, but it stands as a potent and humbling sign of our role as co-creator with God. We have called it into being, a new species of creature, representing both our desire to relieve suffering and our power to inflict it, our choices for death and for life, writ very small and very large in its tiny, patented body. For not only is it an experimental subject, but also property bought and sold, if for the best of purposes. We wrestle with our difficult necessities. How shall we, its makers, be holy?

Satan said to Jesus, "If you are the Son of God, command these stones to become bread. Feed yourself. Feed all the hungry of the world. Rearrange it all for our convenience and your desire." And Jesus answered that life comes from the mouth of God, not only from loaves of bread. Holiness comes from aligning himself with God's will and God's desire. As for us, it is a path of humility and attention.

Satan said to Jesus on the mountain heights looking down at the kingdoms of the world, "All this I will give to you, if you will worship me." Our temptations may be more subtle, more difficult to sort out from our vocations, more convoluted than those which have been set down as Jesus' particular temptations for power, for influence, for status, for wealth.

Our diplomats, with those of other nations, struggle to pull together a patchwork peace in Eastern Europe, in the Middle East, and elsewhere. At times we seek to preserve our national interests; at times we act out of concern for the well being of others; at times our motivations are cloudy. How shall we, who see few ways to prevent the carnage of ethnic cleansing save by military action, be holy? Which suffering will we allow, which prevent and which inflict? And what are our motivations, explicit and hidden, in choosing as we do? And in our personal lives, in our workplaces, how shall we be holy in sorting out our ambiguous motivation for advancement and accomplishment, for change, for security and productivity? How often do we call to mind the One we worship, and God's call to holiness, in all the small decision-making of our workaday lives?

For us, the tempter's hands may offer not only what we do not have but want, but also the chance to keep what we have already obtained. How shall we be holy in our choosing?

On the battlements of the temple, Satan said to Jesus, "If you are the Son of God, throw yourself down. Let the angels save you, to show your power and privilege." How is it that we flaunt our magical sense of limitless power? Perhaps by indulging our bodies in ways that injure our health? Perhaps by consuming the resources our children will need tomorrow, in the assumption that the knowledge of the next generation will be able to remedy our exploitation? Perhaps by exposing ourselves to the continual violent titillation of our culture, assuming that images and thought have no power to transform us? How shall

97

we be holy, knowing that we fear death and desire security and satisfaction?

In Christ Jesus, God's grace allows us to become holy, Paul tells the Roman Christians, and us. In Jesus, God has taken on the stuff of creation—flesh, matter, body—and sanctified it utterly, reconciling it to Godself. In Jesus there is no distance left between the Creator and the Creation—all are made One. In Jesus, no depth of earthly suffering is left outside God's experience. In the Eucharist which is for us the living body of the Holy One, into which we are incorporating, in one Body, ourselves, the entire creation is made to shine with holiness. So for us who eat and drink God, the universe flows with sacramental power to communicate God to us. Its atoms dance with God's vitality and purpose in which we share. We begin to look for and find God in every corner of it, hidden in its cells, sparkling between its stars in its mysterious unceasing music.

Apprehending God in the whole creation, and fed by God's nurturing presence, we return to our choices as those who seek to discern good and evil with great care, with great tenderness and compassion, with great attention and penitence. We seek to live lives of holiness step by step, knowing our frailty, the limits of our understanding, the truth of our finitude. We know that we cause suffering, sometimes must, and we seek never to pass by the suffering of the world's creatures with averted faces; we look, we mourn, we try to heal and help. We know that the waters of the earth which we pollute become unfit for baptism— that they no longer are able to be signs and sacraments of God's new life—so we seek to keep them clear. Those from whom we steal become our enemies so that we cannot speak to one another of God and be heard, and so we seek to be makers of peace. We recognize that the violence we take into ourselves becomes written in our souls and memories as usual and familiar and acceptable, and so we seek to exorcise its power with the foolish gentleness of the Gospel.

The path of holiness opens before us when we see the broken bread of Christ's Table, the circle of the whole earth, broken by sin and in need of repair, broken open by surprising grace and suffused with the new life of the risen Christ, broken to be shared and incorporated into our bodies as our bodies return to be incorporated back into the earth, broken open to reveal the light of God's mystery to those with eyes to see and hearts to receive.

The path of holiness opens before us when we desire God more than all the world.

A story: there was a disciple who, each day, would ask his teacher the same questions, " "How shall I be holy? How shall I find God?" And each day he would receive the same answer," "Through desire."

"But I desire God with all my heart, don't I? Then why haven't I found God?"

One day the teacher and the student were bathing in the river. The teacher caught the young man by his hair and pushed his head underwater while the poor lad struggled to break loose. The next day, the teacher spoke first, "Why did you struggle so when I held your head under water?"

"Because I was desperate for air."

"When you are given grace to gasp for God the way you gasped for air, you will find holiness. You will find God." Amen.

Lent 2   John 3:1-17

Sermon As Gift

Ann Duffy

It's funny, but after more than fifteen years in the ministry, I know less about preaching than I did when I was a seminary student. Why might one sermon seem to have a visible effect upon it hearers and another might not? There are those sermons on which I lavish great amounts of time and come Sunday morning worship time I have my doubts. There are some Sundays when I am in the middle of delivering what I believe is a clear message and I look out over the congregation and see blank looks. It causes me no little concern. Why select one approach to the text over another? What objective do I have in mind? I recall one seminary professor telling us that some sermons backfire, some roll over and play dead, some miss their mark, some limp into sermon oblivion, and some, some have a profound effect upon their hearer. Why?

This week was the usual busy kind—meetings, counseling, phone messages to return, disagreements to settle between the groups who use our space. I had planned to begin my sermon early this week, but, as usual, Saturday came and I had not even thought about the text. Most Saturdays are like that. How many Sunday mornings I have felt less than eager to enter the pulpit, feeling ill prepared to deliver a sound, meaningful message. But I do, and when the service is over and I stand and greet each one of you at the door, inevitably one of you will shake my hand and say, "Good sermon, Pastor, just what I needed." "What?" I want to call you back and say. " Why? What did I say that you needed to hear?" But I usually retreat to my office and offer thanks to the Spirit who enabled someone to get what they needed.

The gospel tells us that it was late one night when one of the religious officials knocked at Jesus' door. His name was Nicodemus. He asked if Jesus had a few minutes to talk because he, Nicodemus, had some questions about something Jesus had said in one of his sermons. Perhaps Jesus was making a mental note as to which sermon Nicodemus was referring. But Nicodemus got right to the point. He said, "Jesus, I've watched you and listened to you these past several months, and I am impressed by what I have seen—water turned to wine, the sick made well, the lame made able to walk, your followers growing with each sermon you deliver. I've heard you speak about this place called 'heaven'. How does one get to this place called heaven?"

After listening to Nicodemus's sincere question, Jesus tells him, "Well, I have three things to say in answer to your questions: first, you must be 'born from above', 'second, you must receive the Holy spirit', and third 'the wind blows where it will'."

That was just like Jesus, ask him a simple question and he gives you an unclear allegorical explanation in response. Nicodemus asks him how to get to heaven and Jesus uses cosmic terms like wind, rebirth, and spirit. Nicodemus came to Jesus to be enlightened and Jesus responds with seemingly impossible expectations. In order to get to heaven, one must be reborn, receptive and open to the Spirit, and in the right place at the right time. I can imagine the look upon Nicodemus's face. Filled with frustration and confusion, Nicodemus asks what appears to be an obvious question. "But how can one enter the womb and be born again?" And Jesus answers, "You are a learned person, Nicodemus, and yet you do not understand?" Perhaps Nicodemus fails to understand Jesus' teaching because Nicodemus only knows what he knows. Nicodemus's world is the secular, physical world. His understanding is limited to that which is tangible. Jesus speaks of spiritual things, and Nicodemus does not understand. And then Jesus tries to clear up Nicodemus's (and our?) confusion. Jesus uses an example from nature, the wind. Jesus implies that not all people will understand his message and be open to the spirit. Because it isn't physical rebirth about which Jesus speaks. It's about being spiritually reborn — born from above. The Greek word Jesus uses for "born again" is *anothen* which means "from top to bottom, from above." One must be "born from above" not "reborn" from the womb. But Nicodemus does not understand because he intellectualizes Jesus' message.

But even today, some Christians misunderstand Jesus' words. There are some well-intentioned Christians who believe Jesus' teaching about "born again" meant that one had to be re-baptized and believe that he/she was then initiated into an elite group of Christians who are then "saved" as distinct from those others who are not saved. There are some who use this text to set themselves apart from all other Christians. They even claim that only Christians can get to the "place" called heaven. They too, like Nicodemus, misunderstand this text. Jesus said, one must be "born from above," born in the spiritual sense, made whole, body and soul, in the Spirit. How does one do this? Well, the way I understand Jesus is that it isn't up to us to do this, it's up to God. Our responsibility is to just be open to the Spirit. Jesus goes on to say that "the wind blows where it will," and I kept wondering just how Jesus translated "wind." I looked up the Greek word again and found that word *pneuma* which is translated "wind or spirit." Although Jesus uses the movement of the wind to explain how uncontrollable and unpredictable the wind is, in so doing he implies that God's spirit is also not under human control or prediction. It is not coincidence that Jesus uses two of the most mysterious, at least in those days, natural occurrences, birth and wind, to explain the workings of God's spirit.

And then Jesus delivers what I believe is the sermon-in-a-nutshell-bottom-line of today's text, ". . . for God so loved the world that God gave . . . " Again back to my basic Greek dictionary. I looked up the word "gave" and found the word *charis* which translates "gift of grace." Can you accept a gift, Nicodemus? And Nicodemus replied, "I don't understand." And Jesus said, "Now you're getting it, Nic, now the light comes on."

Like many of us, Nicodemus was a skeptic. He intellectualized everything he believed or he couldn't accept it as truth. Nicodemus wanted to know what he could do to get to heaven. Is there a book to read, a technique to learn, more laws to obey? And Jesus answered in essence, "You can't do anything." It's God who does the "doing." Like the wind, grace and God's spirit, are gifts God gives freely to any who would receive them.

I don't know how God works, or why one sermon hits home and another seems to flop. I guess it's like the wind, fragile, unpredictable, uncontrollable, like the spirit of God moving among us. Although I don't know who or why, I believe it, because it has been my experience in my own life that God's spirit does act in our human affairs if we are open to it.

One Sunday as I stood on the church steps after worship, a young man shook my hand and with unabashed honesty remarked, "I don't know, Pastor, I didn't get a thing out of your message this morning." To which I replied, "Oh well, the wind blows where it wills."

Lent 3   John 4:1-15; 39-42

Meeting Jesus At The Well

Virginia Lambert Mason

It was noon. The sun was blazing down. The air was dry and full of dust. There was no noise in the midday heat, no noise of shouting merchants or children at play, only the buzzing of flies made lazy by the heat. Tired from walking, a man sat down in the shade of the well.

It was a tired Jesus, a bone-weary and parched-with-thirst Jesus, who sat at the well that day at Sychar, in Samaria.

Jesus sat, waiting, while his friends went to buy provisions.

Jesus sat, waiting, shoulders hunched and head bowed under the burden of his disciples' concern. They had set off some time ago, apprehensive and scared, worried over how they would find food in a foreign land, enemy territory at that.

Jesus sat, waiting, hoping someone would come along with rope and bucket so that he could ask for a drink to quench his thirst. A woman passed that way. She approached the well tentatively, hoping to draw water and be gone without notice, without being harassed there. She saw the stranger sitting with his back against the stones of the well. Apprehensive, she approached, unsure what to expect, unsure how he would react to her presence. And Jesus said, "Give me a drink."

Like the story of Nicodemus, this story presents a one-on-one encounter, an "inquirer's class" of one, uncomplicated by the presence of the disciples or a curious crowd. And like the story of Nicodemus, we are immediately aware of images, images which carry the story along with their layers of meaning.

But the setting couldn't be more unlike the Nicodemus encounter. Geography is important here! Nicodemus, a prominent Pharisee, a ruler among the Jews, was a person of stature and importance. His journey across town to meet Jesus in the middle of the night signifies both the appeal of Jesus' message to the religious establishment and their apparent hard-heartedness. Nicodemus left Jesus after that first meeting confused and troubled.

At the opposite end of the social spectrum is the woman who meets Jesus at the well in Samaria. She is a woman, a nobody. She has no name, no social stature at all. We guess from the fact that she has come to draw water at the harshest hour of the day that she is a pariah among her people. As the story unfolds, the narrator hints at a shameful past, five husbands and "another to whom she is not married." Jesus tells her about her life, "telling her all she had ever done." But worst of all, she is a Samaritan Jew, a detail which signifies complete enmity from the Judean Jews. Nicodemus and Jesus, both of Judea, at least share a social context, a set of religious values and traditions. What Jesus and the woman share is a history, a long history, of hatred and mutual mistrust.

It is a remarkable story, and familiar: his challenge, her sarcastic reply; his puzzling statements, her sincere questions as she struggles to understand him; his invitation to drink living water, and her conviction, finally, that Jesus is the Savior of the World.

The story has got to be one of the best loved and most familiar of the Gospels. It is a story of barrier-breaking, of profound acceptance as Jesus, a male, a Jew, a rabbi, encounters and converses with a Samaritan woman, an outcast of her own people, at Jacob's Well outside the city gate.

It is a profound story.

For women, it has always stood as a proof text to which we hold fast against the oppressive texts elsewhere in the Bible. It is a story, at its root, which proclaims the utter seriousness with which Jesus took women: that Jesus recognized women as humans, as dialogue partners, equally worthy of his attention and his consideration. These are simple truths, undeniable and accessible from a plain reading of the text. But this is not a simple story.

Lest you begin to squirm in your seats this morning, fearing that you will be asked to listen to or maybe even admit the female perspective of this morning's text, I'd like to reassure you. This is not just good news for women. Nor is it "good news" for all God's people with its clear affirmation of the full humanity and worth of women. The story has a much broader meaning if we listen carefully to the writer, if we hear it in context, if we watch for the signs which are there. For this is a complicated story. It is a narrative bursting with images and inviting interpretation on a number of levels.

The structure of this story follows a familiar pattern. I don't think we're supposed to miss the hints that alert the listener—"Listen up! This is going to be one of those stories about a man and a woman meeting at a well" For Jesus' listeners, the familiar pattern goes like this: a man goes to a well; he meets a maiden there; they talk; she returns home to tell her people about him; eventually she invites the man home to dinner and a wedding takes place.

107

We've heard the story many times before. A well was the meeting place of Isaac and Rebekkah, of Jacob and Rachel, the place where Moses met Zipporah. Wells are places of meeting, sources of life-sustaining water, solemn and public places where covenants were witnessed and sealed. It is no coincidence that this encounter takes place at a well. And no coincidence that we are intended to recall Jacob.

For it is not just any well, outside any city. This is **the** well, the Well of Jacob, as the author reminds us no less than three times in the first twelve verses. Jacob, you will remember, was the son of Isaac, the son of Abraham. Abraham is the common ancestor of all Jews, Christians, and Muslims. Jacob, who was renamed "Israel," met Rachel at **this** well, and married her, then fathered the twelve sons whose names are those of the twelve tribes of Israel. Now remember how important geography is to this story. Jacob, father of all Jews, was a northerner.

Judean Jews, the southern branch, and the Samaritan Jews of the north had been mortal enemies since the argument six centuries earlier over **who** would rebuild the Temple and **where** it would be built. Two rival cities were built, Shechem and Jerusalem. Two temples were constructed, the fabulous Temple of Solomon in Jerusalem, and the other on Mount Gezerim, the legendary meeting place between heaven and earth. The dispute had finally come to a climax in 107 BC when the Southerners destroyed the shrine at Mount Gezerim and razed the city of Shechem.

From the well at Sychar in the "field Jacob gave Joseph," Jesus and the woman of Samaria could look across and see the ruined Samaritan sanctuary on Mount Gezerim. Do you begin to get the picture? Like the Protestants and Catholics in Northern Ireland, like the Serbs and Croats in Yugoslavia, like the Tutsis and Hutus in Rwanda, like the Christians and Muslims and Jews in present-day Palestine, only cultures of common ancestry seem capable of spawning such a deep hatred that it can last over centuries.

The result of this hostility in the first century was a deep, seemingly insurmountable hatred. Although Samaria lay directly between Galilee in the north and Judea in the south, Judean Jews on pilgrimage would cross the Jordan River and travel around Samaria rather than ever set foot in enemy territory.

So the story begins with the simple sentence, "Jesus left Judea and started back to Galilee. But he had to go through Samaria." He had to go **through Samaria**. He **had** to go through Samaria? That's what it says. But I believe Jesus **chose** to go through Samaria. No self-respecting, observant, Judean would choose to go by way of Samaria. But the story says Jesus had to. His "necessity" required bridging an enormous chasm.

Although we can fruitfully read this story on a purely human level, to do so misses the point, misses the richness. To mine the depths of the story, it is necessary to read the signs: the "living water" which Jesus offers is of far greater life-sustaining value than mere water from this well. The water Jesus offers, even Jacob could not supply. The "true worship" Jesus describes is worship "in spirit and in truth," not fixed in any particular geographical place. Neither Mount Gezerim nor in the Temple of Jerusalem.

Without resolution of the hostility between the two estranged nations, the Jews of Samaria and the Jews of Judea, the story is without purpose. It concludes with the happy, although surprising, ending of this woman, the nameless Samaritan woman, becoming the first apostle. "Many Samaritans from that city believed in him because of the woman's testimony." She is truly a messenger of good news. She came to the well with her clay jar, ready to fill it. She received the living water and it transformed her. Now in her joy she turns from Jesus to share what she has received.

It was midday and the sun was blazing down. The air was muggy, making the clothes cling to their bodies. The seven-year-old girl, tired from a day of shopping with her aunt, suddenly spotted a drinking fountain and pulled loose from her aunt's hand, running toward it. With a sharp intake of breath her aunt broke into a run, snatched her away, and called out to her, "Don't child! It's a white's only fountain!" And Jesus said, "Give me a drink."

It was the middle of the night. It was winter and the room was never warm enough, no different from the other sections of the city hospital. Even the pile of fraying blankets did nothing to keep out the chill, which caused the man's body to shake all over. He had lost his small business, then his health. He had no money. Eventually he had lost touch with his wife back in Haiti, and now he was alone. He lay awake, knowing he was dying, afraid, wanting his wife, wanting someone to hold his hand. But there was no one because he was poor and dying of AIDS. It was midday and the sun was blazing down. And Jesus said, "Give me a drink."

It was evening, and the day had been long and hard. With several inches of old snow on the ground, walking two miles to the unemployment office over unplowed, broken sidewalks had been laborious, tiring work. The two miles back to the rooming house had taken all afternoon. Would it never end? Would there ever be a job, self-respect? Would he ever see his children again? That other life seemed like so long ago. Someone produced a bottle of cheap booze, and the others began to help themselves, first one gulp, then another, passing the bottle around. The tiredness seemed to recede, things seemed easier, reality less stark. Until all at once someone let fly an insult he didn't really mean, but the result was immediate: curses, fists, fighting, knives, a bleeding wound. It was midday and the sun was blazing down. And Jesus said, "Give me a drink."

It was the middle of the afternoon. The sun shone weakly, giving little warmth. Though it was still the middle of the day, the town center was deserted, shoppers had gone home, business people were out of view in their warm offices. It had been a long day, riding in a cab to first one church and then another. Sometimes there had been a friendly face, sometimes only a locked door. It seemed like forever since her husband of fifteen years had come home at four o'clock that morning, drunk, angry, and gotten into a fight over nothing. That explained her swollen face, the blackened eyes, the crusted, tender lips. While hitching a ride from the shopping plaza, she was offered fifty bucks by a well-dressed businessman to give him what he wanted. She jumped out of the car at the next stop light. No thanks, mister! I just need a little help, a little money so I can take my Joey and get out of here, get to my sister's down in Maryland. It was midday and the sun was blazing down. And Jesus said, "Give me a drink."

Many are the forms of exclusion practiced today, in the community, in the church, in the world. Hatred and imagined

111

difference keep us from sharing the Living Water, keep us from receiving the Living Water when it is offered. What does the story mean? Jesus was, above all, a reconciler. Seeking to heal division, Jesus calls us to remember our commonality. Not waiting until a stranger comes into our midst, but taking extraordinary measures, going out of our way.

Jesus went to Samaria because he had to. Jesus said, "Give me a drink." And Jesus said, "Everyone who drinks of the water that I give them will never be thirsty. The water that I will give them will become in them a spring of water gushing up to eternal life." COME! COME TO THE WATER!

Lent 4   1 Samuel 16:1-13

Chosen[1]

Ruth Brandon Minter

Samuel—chosen by God to anoint kings. To anoint was to perform a ceremony with oil to mark a person as the one chosen by God to be king.

In the passage we read today, Samuel has a problem. It wasn't long ago that he did what God said and anointed Saul as king and told Saul God's orders. Now God is telling Samuel that Saul never obeyed God and God no longer wants Saul as king. Samuel knows that again he must be the pointer to identify the new king. That is the story we are reading today. Listen well because God's choice is a big surprise.

> The Lord said to Samuel, "How long will you grieve over Saul? I have rejected him from being king over Israel. fill your horn with oil and set out; I will send you to Jesse the Bethlehemite, for I have provided for myself a king among his sons." Samuel said, "How can I go? If Saul hears of it, he will kill me." And the Lord said, "Take a heifer with you, and say, 'I have come to sacrifice to the Lord.' Invite Jesse to the sacrifice, and I will show you what you shall do; and you shall anoint for me the one whom I name to you." Samuel did what the Lord commanded, and came to Bethlehem. The elders of the city came to meet him trembling, and said, "Do you come peaceably?" He said, "Peaceably; I have come to sacrifice to the Lord; sanctify yourselves and come with me to the sacrifice." and he sanctified Jesse and his sons and invited them to the sacrifice.

113

When they came, he looked on Eliab and thought, "Surely the Lord's anointed is now before the Lord." But the Lord said to Samuel, "do not look on his appearance or on the height of his stature, because I have rejected him; for the Lord does not see as mortals see; they look on the outward appearance, but the Lord looks on the heart." then Jesse called Abinadab, and made him pass before Samuel. He said, "Neither has the Lord chosen this one." Then Jesse made Shammah pass by. And he said, "Neither has the Lord chosen this one." Jesse made seven of his sons pass before Samuel, and Samuel said to Jesse, "The Lord has not chosen any of these." Samuel said to Jesse, "Are all your sons here?" and he said, "There remains yet the youngest, but he is keeping the sheep." and Samuel said to Jesse, "Send and bring him; for we will not sit down until he comes here." He sent and brought him in. Now he was ruddy, and had beautiful eyes, and was handsome. The Lord said, "Rise and anoint him for this is the one." Then Samuel took the horn of oil, and anointed him in the presence of his brothers; and the spirit of the Lord came mightily upon David from that day forward. Samuel then set out and went to Ramah.

It looks to me as though even in ancient times—a very long time before Christ—God liked to choose people whom the world thought were of little importance. In this case it was a choice from among the sons of Jesse.

First, there was Eliab—tall and handsome. If it were an occasion for choosing a husband, there would be women who would say, "Yes, indeed, I'd like to be with him!" but God said "No, I see what is in his heart."

What about Abinadab? God said no. And Shammah? God said no to him also. One by one, father Jesse brought seven sons to Samuel. All of them were more or less grown and were thought of as men. But God said "no" to each one of them.

The one God chose, the eighth son, still quite young, was a child who stayed far from the house tending sheep. He was young enough that his father didn't even think of him when Samuel came to choose among his sons. The Bible says David was "a handsome, healthy, young man, and his eyes sparkled!" As we read further in the story of David as told in the books of Samuel, we learn that, while still young, David was well known as a skilled singer and player of the harp. Later he was respected as an excellent soldier.

But how surprised everyone was. God sent Samuel to anoint this "boy" in front of his many older brothers so that all of them would understand that, although young, he would command all of them.

God's ways are indeed difficult to predict. We must always stay open to new possibilities and even surprises.

Of course even Samuel, the old man in today's story, was chosen by God when he was very young. His parents turned him over as servant to a holy man when he was still a child, and while he was still quite small, he had experienced being startled out of his sleep three times in one night by someone calling "Samuel!" Each time the boy went to the old man he served, but he had not called. Finally the old man told the boy what answer to make if he were called again. That made it possible for God to use the boy to get an important message to the old man and to the people of those days.

Again—a surprise—God using a child to carry an important message? How often it is that we do not listen to what children are saying. If God were to do this today, I don't know whether we'd even hear! Our society today, as in the time of Samuel and David, is a society that considers wisdom and leadership the prerogative of older people. And it is true that older people often do know what is good. They should be heard.

But God's ways are difficult to predict. We must stay open to new possibilities and even surprises.

Let's think about others in the Bible whom God chose. Abraham—in this case it was an old man who was chosen, a very old man. He had lived his whole life in one place, as a farmer. His wife had given up the idea of having children because she was also old. They should have been well into retirement, letting the young folks assume most responsibilities, but that is not what we are told. God chose this very couple to be father and mother of a people, leading them in wandering from place to place in search of the "promised land"—land promised by God. When the call came, Sarah and Abraham couldn't believe their ears. Them? Have children? Sarah burst out laughing. Them? Leave the home they had always known? But in the end they believed and accepted.

God's ways are difficult to predict. We must always stay open to new possibilities and even surprises.

In the New Testament, we discover the same truth through Jesus—God's will in that part of the story is also full of surprises.

Consider Jesus, himself—a child in a carpenter's family—nobody special—a family similar to yours. And when Jesus began his ministry, look at who he picked for disciples. Were they important people? Educated people? Famous leaders? Not at all. He chose several fishermen, a tax collector, a man who had been part of a group that had revolted against the colonial government, and others whom he picked up here and there. They were ordinary people—nobody particular in the eyes of the world. But they were called, and they responded, and after Jesus' death and resurrection, the birth of the early Christian church was in their hands.

God's ways are difficult to predict. We must always stay open to new possibilities and even surprises.

Another choice by Jesus was even more of a surprise to people of his day. Who was it that Jesus sent to evangelize the Samaritan people—that neighboring people treated with so much contempt by the peoples among whom Jesus was born? Do you remember that time when Jesus was tired and thirsty after a long day of walking from place to place and teaching? He stopped by a well while his disciples went to buy some food in the town. There at the well, he talked to a Samaritan woman, and a sinful one at that. After a long discussion with her, he sent her to tell what she had learned to the other Samaritans—and she did. Now in those days even the fact of him speaking to a Samaritan was most surprising, but it was so surprising as to be almost beyond belief that the person to whom he spoke was also a woman—and worse than that, a woman whose many sins were well-known. But she was the very one whom he chose to evangelize the Samaritan people.

God's ways are difficult to predict. We must always stay open to new possibilities and even surprises.

Finally, let us remember the Apostle Paul. He wasn't always a follower of Jesus. He wasn't always called Paul. He began life as Saul—like the ancient king. But this New Testament Saul hunted down the followers of Christ. And when he caught them he ordered them killed. He represented the colonial power in trying to close the new churches.

But Jesus got into Saul's heart—and transformed him completely. Who would think that the man who killed Christians would become the most important person in the initial carrying of the Gospel to lands beyond Israel? Who could imagine that this man who persecuted the early church in Israel would be founder of so many churches outside Israel, indeed suffering many calamities, even prison and death while following the way of Jesus. But this bad man, Saul, was chosen and answered.

God's ways are difficult to predict. We must always stay open to new possibilities and even surprises.

What new possibilities and surprises could God present us with today? Do we have older people capable of receiving orders from God to guide us in new directions, perhaps even leaving the comfort of having everything in the church done "the way it's always done?" I don't know. We must stay open.

Do we have young people whom God might use as the mouthpiece to us of wise words? I don't know. But we must stay open.

Do we have sinners and people who have mistreated believers and churches in our society? Might God choose one of them to do God's work in Mozambique—perhaps together without a church? I don't know. But we must stay open.

Do we have women whom God could accost and confront with the "good news" and call to leave her usual work to become a church worker? I don't know. But we must stay open.

God's ways are difficult to predict. We must always stay open to new possibilities and even surprises.

When we pray, it should not be just thanks and requests. We should also listen. We must listen to the silence, listen inside our hearts, listen for God and let God speak to us. When it is we who are always talking, we are not able to hear either our neighbor or God. And sometimes it is through a neighbor that God is trying to reach us.

We are in the process of building a new congregation here. The church is the people. It is a believing people, a people who accept Jesus and serve God. We are in search of God's will for our community. We each have ideas. Next week, at ten o'clock, before worship, in a classroom in the back, we will probe to bring those ideas to the surface for the future of this church. I believe God will show us the road of strength and faithfulness. I don't know where the most important ideas will come from, anybody here could turn out to be the mouth of God trying to communicate with us. We must listen well to all ideas from all people. Let nobody think herself or himself unimportant. Everybody over twelve years of age should participate in the upcoming discussion about our future. Together, with the help of God, we will develop this new church.

But we must always remember; God's ways are difficult to predict. We need to stay open to new possibilities and even surprises.

Lent 5   John 11:1-8; 17-44
                                            Ezekiel 37:1-14

Matters Of Life And Death

Mary Susan Gast

There comes a time in the lives of each of us when, "Smile, God loves you" just doesn't hack it any more.

Not that it isn't a true statement. A needed-to-be-heard statement. At times a welcome statement. But there are moments when no easily uttered words can speak to the anguish of the human heart.

That is the situation in which we find both Martha and Mary in today's Gospel story.

Martha hears that Jesus is coming—now, four days after Lazarus has died. She is living within the blankness, the ache, the emptiness that surround the death of someone who has been so close. Walter Scott wrote when his wife died, that a kind of cloud of stupidity hung about him, as if all were unreal--what people seemed to be doing and saying. "All is unreal": this permanent absence of a spouse; this hollow emptiness of arms that once cradled a baby; this great gaping lack of a friend, or, for Martha, a brother.

So with this cloud of stupidity hanging about her, Martha goes out to meet Jesus. And she can't believe that he wasn't there when he was needed. "Rabbi, if you had been here, my brother would not have died. Oh, but you are here now. Well, even now I know that whatever you ask from God, God will give you. Do something, Jesus. Make it all come out right. Let me waken to find it's all been a nightmare." And Jesus responds, "Your brother will rise again."

That is not what Martha needs: some hope for some kind of resurrection some day far off in some future somewhere. "Nice try, Jesus. I know that he'll be there at the resurrection at the end of time. But what about now?"

What about now? What about the loss of power, loss of relationship, loss of hope that death brings? What about death—this ultimate exile from all that is familiar?

These are important questions which Martha raises on behalf of us all.

So often, you know, we Christians really would like to gloss over that part of the life of Christ. We would prefer a Savior who took us on a more pleasant route to salvation. We find ourselves uncomfortable and almost embarrassed by the events surrounding Jesus' death: betrayal, physical torture, psychological trauma, spiritual agony, and finally not even a gracious and peaceful death, but an unjust execution. Not that we want to skip Good Friday entirely, but we'd rather skim across it. And we sometimes find ourselves explaining, with an almost childlike brightness and eagerness, "Yes Jesus died on Good Friday. But he rose on Sunday! It all came out all right."

My mother's mother is Slovak. She grew up in a remote village in the foothills of the Carpathian Mountains, virtually untouched by the nineteenth century, let alone the twentieth.

By the time I came along she was an American citizen. It was significant to me in my childhood that my grandparents were the first in our family circle to own a television. I recall that one Saturday night in the 1950s, I was at my grandparents' home watching the film version of Dracula on "Shock Theater" and becoming more and more frightened in the process. The adults joined me in the shadowy living room as the program was concluding.

At the movie's end I turned around, seeking some assurance that it was, after all, just a movie, not to be taken seriously, and so forth.

Instead, my grandmother looked at me and said solemnly, her Eastern European accent remarkably similar to Bela Lugosi's speech pattern, "Ees all true!"

Well, Grandma had done some mixing of folklore and facts. But when it comes to teaching about the reality of death, John the Evangelist has not garbled it. The Gospel writer and Martha, and Mary, and Lazarus are all here to play grandma to us today, and tell us, "It **is** all true."

Death is real. "There's a foul odor in the tomb," Mary says. Poverty is real. Racism is real. Sexism is real. Violence is real. Don't tell me it's going to come out all right. What are you doing about it?

And Jesus responds to Martha. "You really believe I'm the one who can do something about it?"

And Martha says, "Of course, You are the clear revelation of God. God's anointed one; God's son." (And the implications in that time and place were that the son was the heir. Not the daughter, not the servant, only the son would inherit the estate and the family name and the authority of the father). "You have it within you to bring forth all of God's love and creativity and to pour it over this wretched situation like a fragrant and healing oil."

"You're right, Martha. Now let me speak with Mary."

So Martha goes to fetch her sister, who has gone out of the tomb to weep many times. And when Mary gets up to go out to talk with Jesus, the other mourners follow her, thinking to accompany her once again to the tomb.

Thus Jesus, looking for Mary, meets up with a sorrowing crowd coming toward him. Seeing them weeping, Jesus is deeply moved and weeps with them.

Why does he weep? Knowing that life is about to be restored to Lazarus, knowing that his friends' lamenting is but minutes away from being transformed into a dance of joy, why does he weep?

I can think of no good reason other than compassion. Compassion. Quite literally it means "to weep with."

So often we imagine God as the cosmic manipulator, or the almighty spectator.[2] You know, there's God sitting up there on some cumulus configuration, saying, "Lets rig up a little flood action in Bangla Desh. How about some hurricanes in Florida? Or 80% unemployment on the Pine Ridge Reservation? Just for fun let's throw some tainted well water into Battle Creek and well, maybe this would be a good day to mess up a computer disc and send false signals to surprise everyone with a nuclear war."

But through the person of Jesus—this window to God—through Jesus, we cannot help but recognize that God is neither aloof observer nor mass murderer. God instead chooses to live and die with us—to share our common lot. Today, in Judea, outside Bethany, Jesus wept. Out of compassion for what his friends were suffering—and what he knows was still ahead of them after this crisis had been resolved—out of compassion, Jesus wept.

123

Just as in a few days, in Jerusalem, out of compassion, Jesus will go to his own death. Jesus knows, when he chose to return to Bethany, that he was re-entering dangerous territory. As his disciples commented, "The Pharisees were about to stone you. You got out just in time—and now you're planning to go back there" Of course he is. He knows that his hour has come. He knows that the moment of the New Creation is at hand. That those bones are going to live. That he is so closely in tune with the loving and creative Spirit of the universe that he will be shown to have power even over the grip of death. He will be glorified by the death of Lazarus. But we must remember that when John the Gospel writer refers to Jesus and glory he does not refer to prestige and honor. In John's way of telling it, "glory" always refers to death. When Jesus is lifted up, he is lifted up on a cross.

As Dorothee Soelle puts it, the cross is the sinful world's answer to attempts at liberation. Whether it is liberation from disease, infirmity, poverty, political oppression, personal sinfulness, a wretched past—whatever. Jesus lived a life of love that sought to free people from burdens that were crushing the life out of them. Such a life of love does not ask for the cross, but inevitably it ends up on the cross.

The cross is the sinful world's answer to a life of love that pours itself out for the despised of the earth, that allies with those who are suffering.

Jesus Christ died for us—Jesus dies with us—because he knows us in our pain. He knows when we feel insignificant. He knows us when we don't have enough money to buy food at the end of the month and our children are hungry. He knows us when we lose our jobs. He knows us when our family tears apart at its straining seams. He knows us when we face the chilling words. "You have cancer." He knows us when our most cherished dreams crumble into ashes. He knows us when we sit alone in impenetrable isolation after our beloved dies. He knows us. He has been there. He has felt our pain and our bitterness. Compassion.

The theologian Thomas Muntzer has said. "If you do not want the bitter Christ, you will eat yourself to death on honey."

Or, to put it another way, without knowledge of life's difficulties, without the pain without the bitterness, without the weeping, the compassion is a charade. Counterfeit. A confection without substance. An ethereal smile that could not survive the stench of the tomb.

But Jesus is there in the tomb, in the strongholds of death itself, at Auschwitz, in Soweto, in El Salvador, on the Gulag, in Bosnia, in Webster Groves, at our kitchen tables. Wherever the forces of death threaten, and coerce and terrorize, Jesus weeps. God weeps.

And through that weeping, through that compassion shown to us, there comes transformation. First, we are transformed. We realize that we are not alone—not in our mourning, or in our joy, or in our quest for liberation and salvation. As we view the suffering of God in Christ, as we view the suffering of Christ in the world, we begin whole. And we come to realize that this God—this life-force of the universe—who has been poured out, this God depends on us. This God calls upon us, just as God called upon Ezekiel to prophesy. God calls upon us to speak and to act, because God has no other voice or hands than ours to act on behalf of those who suffer and die, to eliminate the causes of suffering, to bring in the reign of God's love and justice and peace on earth.

We are transformed. We see that our one-ness with God, with love, with all creation is indissoluble. We have learned God's great lesson—that there can never be true joy for me until you, too, are encompassed in joy's vast embrace.

When we undergo such transformation of vision and of understanding, then it is that the miracle of new life happens. We hear the summons to our self-confidence, to our boldness, to our strength. We are not to stay and rot in the tomb. Inside our tombs engulfed by death, the words of empowerment come to us, "Lazarus, come out." When we are wrapped in our cloud of stupidity, immobilized by grief, hobbled by fear, by poverty, by oppression, blinded by old guilts, the voice cuts through, "Unbind her, let her go."

And we know that we are free. Freed from death's terrible isolations. Freed from being trapped within our own decaying skin. Freed for a new life. Different from what went before. Out of nothing we have once again become something. Created in love, mended in love, reborn in love—again and again.

Oh yes, these bones shall live.

Lent 6/ Passion Sunday   Matthew 26:14-27; 66

When The Cheering Stops

Susan L. Boone

A couple of weeks ago I explained the lectionary and how it forced me to deal with scripture that I might be tempted to pass over. I have to say that I was somewhat disconcerted when I first read this piece from the gospel of Matthew. Somehow I expected the passage for today to be about Jesus' triumphant entry into Jerusalem. It's Palm Sunday after all and I wanted celebration, I wanted hosannas, crowds and rejoicing. But in fact it's Passion Sunday as well and what I found was this story from Matthew. I felt as though I had been cheated.

"I don't want to hear this," I said, "I don't want to deal with this. Give me back the parade and the palms." But instead I got this familiar tragic story. This story of alienation, desertion and betrayal, of pain and suffering, of humiliation and death by crucifixion. It's not a pretty picture. We see ourselves mirrored in the story and wonder which person we would be.

We don't like downers, we don't like to hear it. We are uncomfortable looking in the mirror. If we had our choice we would skip over this part, we would picture ourselves as members of the cheering crowd, palms in hand, and go directly from there to the resurrection. Forget the tough stuff, forget the weeping and the wailing, shove it under the rug.

We find the road to Jerusalem not much to our liking, because the road to Jerusalem is hazardous, it's dim and full of holes, forks, and hairpin turns. We discover that when we

127

honestly practice our Christianity we do it at great risk. What happened to the warm and fuzzy stuff? What happened to "Away In the Manger?" To "Jesus Loves Me This I know"? To the star? All the animals? The cozy family gathered around the manger? But the heavenly hosts seem to have packed up their wings, the shepherds have gathered their sheep and along with the magi have returned home. The crowds have suddenly become silent, and out of the silence come the cries of agony and despair. Out of the silence comes the weeping. I am reminded of our own civil rights marches and those in South Africa, peace marches that suddenly explode with violence and death.

What happens when the cheering stops? The story is familiar, it haunts us daily. People are crucified one way or another every day, all we have to do is look at the paper or turn on the news to know that in every corner of our world there is this same story. Stories of oppression and death, of betrayal, of pain, of hatred and violence. We don't like to hear about what happens when the cheering stops, we hold our hands over our ears and hope it will go away. We don't like to be reminded because somewhere deep inside of us we are afraid that we might, in some unknowing way, have contributed to it. We wonder what we would have done at Gethsemane.

Next week is the good news, today is the passion story, and as Christians we can't skip it. We need somehow to recognize it, to talk about it, to come to terms with it and put it into some kind of perspective. Throughout the gospels, but especially here in the passion story, Jesus **is** all of the poor and the oppressed of the world. He **is** the parts of ourselves who are oppressed and

who suffer. We are reminded here that the gospel never promises us a rose garden, never tells us that it's easy, it never tells us
to relax and put our feet up and be comfortable. We are reminded here that it's a difficult way, this road to Jerusalem. That
there are lessons to be learned and at the end of it Jesus asks us
all "Could you not keep awake one hour? Is that so much to
ask, to keep awake just one hour? To bear witness with me?"
Jesus does not ask us to suffer with him nor does he want us to
suffer, but he asks only that we stand in solidarity with him and
protest the systems that produce and condone oppression and
suffering; that we do not sit in silence and inaction; or that we
permit institutionalized violence to wreak havoc in the world.
That's all! That's all?

Is that so much to ask?

A couple of week ago I was with a group of friends who
worship together regularly. We were in an upper room, as it
were, celebrating International Women's Day. We gathered at
an alter, around which were nine baskets of bread, each from a
different culture.[3] We ate tortillas and black bread. We ate
matzo and pita, rice cakes, corn bread and fried bread, and as
we passed the baskets around, we sang. We sang in Spanish, in
Yugoslavian, in Japanese, in Arabic, in Hebrew, in English and
in a Native American dialect. We sang and ate and we remembered. We remembered the Hispanic women of the Americas
who have lived and died in times of persecutions and Hispanic
women of the United States who struggle to live in two cultures.
We remembered the women of Bosnia who have been raped and
who have lost children in the violence and fighting. We remembered our Judeo-Christian past and six million Jews who died in
the Holocaust and those who survived. We remembered Muslim

women caught in the crossfire of national and religious strife, the people of Japan who are still living in the fallout of Hiroshima and Nagasaki, the Japanese-Americans who were interned here in the United Sates during World War II. We remembered those who struggled against slavery, the indigenous people of the Americas whose endurance and strength enabled them to survive. Finally we ate day old bread in remembrance of all those who are homeless or living on the edge, and peanut butter and jelly sandwiches to remind us of the children, the future of the world, our hope for peace and the bringers of joy. We ate in a circle, we sang, we remembered, and we wept.

A friend, whom I was driving home afterwards, asked, "What happened to the celebration? We were suppose to be celebrating."

What happens when the cheering stops?

And yet we cannot be satisfied with just remembering, because when the cheering stops, we find ourselves in the midst of this stark story of Jesus of Nazareth, in the midst of the agony and the betrayal. We find ourselves asking questions for which there are no answers. We find Jesus asking us to be in solidarity with the poor and oppressed and the betrayed. We find Jesus asking "Can you not wait with me one hour? Is that so much to ask? I ask not that you suffer with me, I ask only that you stand in solidarity with me. Do not desert me, do not suffer for me, but protest. Challenge the culture and the systems that enslave, that create and condone violence and oppression. Is that so much to ask?"

We stand in solidarity with our friends every day, but Jesus asks that we stand with him, and by doing so we stand with all those crucified people around the globe. With the starving in

Africa, with the women in Sarajevo, with the homeless on our streets, with all those without hope in our world.

Where is the celebration here? Where is the resurrection? For now, it is only in standing together in an attempt to hold all of the peoples of the earth in love and in hope. As we approach Holy Week, we must ask ourselves some hard questions. Where would we be in Gethsemane? Were we there? Where are we standing? Are we awake or are we asleep? When Jesus asks "Can you not wait one hour with me? Do not desert me, stand with me this one hour? Is that so much to ask?"

What is our answer? For it is when the cheering stops, that the weeping begins.

So be it.

John 19:23-27

A Mother And A Son

Karen E. McArthur

Watching my son die was the hardest thing I have ever had to endure. Children are not supposed to die before their parents. I felt helpless, standing there, watching the life drain from this beautiful, loving, life-giving man, seeing his almost-emaciated body becoming motionless, his skin becoming more and more pale, his hands and feet wounded with ugly sores, his eyes becoming hollow and distant.

This is not the son I knew. He used to be so vibrant and alive, in such great shape from all of his energetic traveling from place to place. He was so good at balancing his life, knowing his need to be rejuvenated by some time apart in prayer, taking time alone with God. I remember how his face would light up when he was doing what he loved to do: reaching out to people, sharing God's healing love with them, passionately speaking of God's new realm of justice and peace. He did that a lot. Too much, it turned out. We tried to warn him—all his life, we tried to warn him that the world would not accept him or his ideals.

When he was first born, the town's attention was on me. Life is never easy for an unmarried pregnant teenager. I knew that this was God's special child, given to the world, through me. Though in the eyes of those around us, I was carrying an illegitimate child, conceived outside of legal marriage, and that was a sin beyond all mention. "The child will amount to nothing," I was told. "You both should be stoned to death." But I knew otherwise. This was God's doing; God would never let that happen. God's word is stronger than human words.

Joseph was a kind and just man, to take me in, to raise my son as if he were his own, to stand up to their disapproval, to their words behind his back, and their words to his face as well. He gave me the courage to continue, to breathe deeply of the gift of life which God had given me. He empowered me to claim what I knew, and not to give in to what others said about me or about our family. I know we passed this on to our son, because I saw that courage in his heart time and time again. We were determined not to pass on to him the failure of others to understand. As he grew up, he knew that he was loved unconditionally, by us and by God, and that he was accepted for who he was, in all his uniqueness. I know we did well, for his compassion for the stranger, the outcast, the lonely was boundless.

Yet as his parents, we saw the pain in his eyes. It is hard when you're not accepted for who you are. No matter how successful you are, or how loved you are in your own home, rejection in any form is painful. He was lucky to have such fine parents, working together, listening for God's word to us as we did our part to raise our son to adulthood. Joseph was older, however, and he is gone now. I miss him, especially now.

My friends rallied around me when Joseph died, supporting me and comforting me. They helped me to find the strength in my own soul, to realize that I would survive. I discovered for myself some of the same courage I had seen in my husband, and was seeing in my growing son. I took a deep breath and decided that I didn't have to be married to survive unless I found just the right man who would continue to support our family, our faith, and our ideals. I could make ends meet on my own if I had to.

My first pregnancy had taken me outside the bounds of society, one more step wouldn't hurt.

I found that my decision allowed me to be open to my friends in new ways, as I first shared the pain of my loneliness, and then the fear that I couldn't support my own family without a husband. We began to share more of ourselves, my friends and I: our joys and delights, our hopes and dreams for a world where people would not become outcasts simply because they did not fit the norm. We shared, as well, our disappointments when our hopes were temporarily dashed. At first, it was just my sister and my friend Mary, the wife of Clopas who were there for me. But recently, that circle of Marys has grown to include two of my son's special friends: Mary from Bethany and Mary from Magdala. We are linked by much more than our common name.

I feel that my son has given me this new understanding of the depth of friendship, as he chose and devoted himself to his own circle of friends. I had hoped that he would find a woman who shared his ideals, that they would marry and raise a family together, that they would escape the stigma of his childhood by creating a conventional family and fading into the fabric of society. But we raised him to follow his heart. As it turned out, that meant that he was more content to live his life with a close-knit group of men, giving his life to healing all who needed it, not just his own children's hurts, feeding all the hungry, not just his own family.

One time, when his brothers and I were concerned about his chosen life and the friends he was keeping, we went and stood outside the place where he was with his friends. We sent a message in to him, "Your mother and your brothers are outside."

But he would have nothing to do with us. "They are not my mother and my brothers. Whoever does the will of God is my mother and my brother and my sister." It was painful at the time. We wanted to protect him, to try to convince him to live within the world as we knew it, within the acceptable limits of our society. And he was rejecting us.

Or was he? Perhaps he was saying, "You're not my only mother and my only brothers. Everyone who does the will of God, everyone who understands God's new realm of justice and peace and inclusion is welcome in my new family." Family is not about biological and legal definitions as much as it is about shared dreams and visions, about honoring and affirming each other. We, his family protected by biological and legal limits, felt rejected, when all he was doing was opening the door wider. The traditional definition of family was too confining for him. It's not surprising. It's what we had taught him all his life.

That's just one example, but it's typical of the way he lived his life. So many flocked to him, for that one healing touch, for that one word of wisdom, for that one glimpse of the God whose word of justice he proclaimed. So many people, too many! The authorities couldn't deal with it. They were threatened; they were afraid of this peasant carpenter from the hill-towns. The religious leaders were worried about their religious institution. His message pushed the edges of the tradition. But if his message had no truth to it, they wouldn't have had to silence him. The political leaders watched the crowds and knew he was gaining influence and leadership at the expense of their own.

We tried to get him to be quiet, not to stir up trouble by being so visible and vocal, but we couldn't. Now I see that if he had become silent just to please us, that would have been even worse. It would have silenced us as well. And so here he is, dying as if he were a common criminal. "He deserved it," people say, "He chose that lifestyle. He should have stayed within the expected norm: married, raised children, been a good Jew, lived within God's law." It's true. Sometimes I wish he had chosen that life. Then he would have been safe, he would be alive, he would be here with me, my son. But that would have killed him even more. To live a life that is not your own, just to please the people around you, would be suffocating and false. If I had done that, if I had said no to God's plan for my life, this child would never have been born and I would probably be a respected member of Jewish society. God calls us to follow our hearts, to live our lives of love and passion. My son lived his life passionately, following God's call to him, even when it cost him his life.

Even here, in these last moments, he remained true to his heart, reaching out to those whom he loved. "Woman," he called out, "Here is your son." I know. You don't have to remind me. He was so close, and yet so distant at the same time. I just wanted to hold him, remembering when he was a little boy, how I could comfort him when he was hurt with a skinned knee or a stomach ache, and again when he was older, helping him to overcome his many disappointments when his friends did not understand him. I just wanted to hold him now, and tell him how sorry I am—how angry I am—that this message of justice that God had given to me and to him was causing him so much pain and suffering. He is very much my son.

As he spoke, he seemed to be motioning to his friend. "Woman, here is your son," he said, indicating his beloved disciple and friend. Then to him, he completed the relationship,

"Here is your mother." I was losing a son, but he was giving his beloved to me. His beloved was losing a friend, a partner in ministry and in life, and he was giving me to him. And so, in my grief, I am welcomed into a new family, one which promises to be open to all people, not confined by legal definitions of who is family and who is not. In our grief, we are rebuilding our lives. In our faith, we are rebuilding the world, with justice and love for all people. In our lives, God's message will never be silenced.

Easter

Easter   Jeremiah 31:1-6

Grace In The Wilderness

Karen E. McArthur

We tend to think of the wilderness somewhat nostalgically, as a faraway, long-ago place of untouched purity, a primeval forest free from the faults of civilization. But it is also a wild and frightening place of unseen dangers and terrifying wild beasts. We like to think that the wilderness has been tamed by technology: we have connected isolated settlements by roads and radio, while we have sheltered vulnerable people from the weather, from wild beasts, and from each other.

These wilderness places are not so threatening any more. The wilderness was real for the Hebrew people, however. Following their escape from slavery in Egypt, they wandered in the wilderness for forty years. There was nowhere else to go. The people grumbled about the lack of food, and remembered that their lives as slaves were not nearly as bad as they had thought. Civilization meant slavery, but freedom in the wilderness wasn't any better.

The wilderness was real for the Pilgrims and Puritans and other early immigrants who crossed the Atlantic. In a 1670 sermon, the Reverend Samuel Danforth described the mission of those people of God as an "Errand into the Wilderness." They had exchanged the comforts of their familiar homes and villages for the unknown hope of the wilderness which they called the "New World."

From Flicker To Flame

The wilderness was real for those who pushed the frontier north and westward into the mountains and beyond. Our own forebears left the comforts of established towns to settle in these hills along the Connecticut River. But now, although there is certainly uninhabited, unfarmed land left, we call it "conservation land" or "national forest." They are familiar hills and valleys to us, complete with charted elevations, drawn out boundaries, and marked trails. Our wilderness has disappeared.

There is another kind of wilderness, one which is very near to us. It is a land where the wild things are, uncultivated and uninhabited, deep and dark, tangled and terrifying; it can be a dangerous place. We don't go there by choice, but by chance, when times of personal tragedy send us wandering aimlessly into our own wildernesses. I am sure that each of you has experienced those times: when you've lost a parent or partner through death or divorce, or when the job which seemed secure is suddenly pulled out from under you, leaving you struggling for your sense of vocation and your sense of self, or when you break off a relationship with someone you thought you really loved, leaving you angry and hurt. Other times, the wilderness is more vague, leaving us to drift and wander, not quite sure where we're headed or what we're looking for or why we're wandering, but knowing that something doesn't seem quite right. When we finally look up, we realize that we don't know where we are. All we know is that we're lost in an unfamiliar place, scared and lonely.

It was this kind of wilderness of grief in which Mary and the women and all the disciples found themselves the weekend Jesus was killed. The man who had been at the center of their lives for many months and many miles, the one who had drawn them

from the familiarity of their lives into the newness of disciple-
ship, the one who had taught them that the kingdom of God was
within them, the one who had brought God to them, so near
they could hear the sound of God's footsteps behind them and
feel the gentleness of God's breath on the back of their necks,
that one—that Jesus—was gone. One evening, he was breaking
bread and sharing the cup with them, and the next day, he was
dead.

And so, in the pre-dawn hours which brought the Sabbath to
its end, the women arrived at the tomb, to see the place which
held the body of the one they loved, the place which made tangible this painful wilderness into which they had suddenly been
exiled. But instead of the tomb they expected, they were surprised by grace in the wilderness.

They were met by an angel who told them that Jesus had
risen and would see them in Galilee. The women "departed
quickly from the tomb with fear and great joy," probably more
fear than joy, for they still didn't know what to make of the
missing body of Jesus. It was only in looking back that they
could recognize the grace which met them there at the tomb. As
Barbara Brown Taylor put it, "When life defies our expectations, we are so quick to assume that all is lost. But the chief
truth of Easter morning is the very opposite: when all seems
lost, all is most truly found."

There is a Russian story of a woman named Babushka, who
carefully painted beautiful, intricate designs on eggshells. All
through the year, she would paint her eggs, getting ready for the
annual festival. She lived in a cottage at the edge of the village,
all alone except for her goose named Rechenka. One day,
Rechenka's flapping wings knocked over the basket of eggs,

breaking them all, a risk, it seems, when one keeps a goose in-
doors. Babushka was crushed. When her beautiful eggs lay
smashed on the floor, all seemed quite lost: her creativity, her
hard work, her chance to win at the festival. She knew that the
eggs could never be put back the way they were. But the next
morning, her own expectations were shattered when she found
that Rechenka had laid a beautiful egg for her; an egg which
was not plain, but already covered with the intricate designs
which provided her livelihood.[1] Babushka found grace in her
wilderness; grace to accept the miracles that came her way.

Salvation comes not in the absence of the wilderness, not in
conquering or subduing it, not in mapping it out and removing
its mysteries, but in learning to live in its midst. And then, it
really is only when we look back that we see that God's grace
had been there all along. We can't plan for that grace, or expect
it, or manufacture it ourselves. Such grace is God's gift to us,
waiting for us. However, we must enter the wilderness to be
surprised by the grace. For it is there that the Easter miracle
makes sense. It's why we can believe in resurrection. We don't
have to see the empty tomb for ourselves, or have a goose lay
intricately decorated eggs at our feet to know that we have
caught a glimpse of God's grace in our wildernesses. All it takes
is a hug from a child, a smile from a new friend, newfound confidence in our capacity to cope, a new talent uncovered, a new
lease on life. The good news of this Easter day is that Christ is
risen, meeting us with grace in all our wildernesses. Thanks be
to God! Amen.

Easter 2
Acts 4:32-35
John 20:19-31

Fear, Doubt, And Faith

Carol K. Towley

The Sunday after Easter is often called "Low Sunday" not only because after the wonderful influx of "Twice a year Christians" on Easter, the half full sanctuary now looks empty or low; but also, for me, and I suspect for many, this Sunday is a real let down. As I experience my own anticipation and excitement of Easter and then go to work on Monday and realize that everything is the same, I come to appreciate how I believe the disciples must have felt that Monday after the crucifixion.

The wonder of the triumphant Palm Sunday, the teachings of Jesus, the growing hope that HE IS THE ONE, the excitement of following this charismatic teacher all slides into the despair of the crucifixion.

Now we go right from Maundy Thursday, Good Friday and Easter vigil straight into Easter Sunday, but I doubt it was that easy for the disciples. And to tell the truth, it is not so easy for me. Every year at the beginning of Lent, I vow to become more disciplined in my daily devotion and prayer life in the hopes that I will experience my own resurrection—that I will come out on the other side of Easter a better person—more loving, more sensitive, more able to follow Jesus' example. And on Monday morning after Easter, the reality hits me that I'm not a different person, and the miraculous changes that I long for, again didn't happen.

When I was younger I think I often got depressed after Easter. I know I was full of questions. What was Easter all about? Who did God want me to be and why didn't God protect me and strengthen me so I could be the kind of Christian that I believed that God wanted me to be? What was the purpose of life? And even, "God are you really up there?"

I can imagine how depressed and ashamed Peter must have felt after the crucifixion. Before things got rough, he was so sure that his love for Jesus would never allow him to deny him, and yet, three times he vowed, "I do not know the man." Apparently he was so ashamed and so sure he had let Jesus down that he isolated himself from the other disciples. In the resurrection story of Mark, the youth in the white robe says. "Fear not; you are looking for Jesus of Nazareth, who was crucified. He has been raised again; he is not here; look, there is the place where they laid him. But go and give this message to his disciples AND TO PETER, "He is going on before you into Galilee; there you will see him, as he told you. "Then they went out and ran away from the tomb, beside themselves with terror."

Fear and shame are closely related feelings that are at the root of depression. When we take inventory of our lives and come up short, it is easy to blame ourselves and to fear that others will also blame us and to fear that God will disown us. I remember the threat growing up that if I was bad or committed any of a long list of sins (and my grandmother had a very long list of sins) I would end up in Hell. For years I really tried to be good, and lived in fear that I wasn't good enough. Until one day in a chancel drama, I played the part of Peter and heard the words of forgiveness for the first time. "Go tell the disciples and tell Peter." Foolish, impetuous, denying Peter was still loved, still worthy, still included. What a relief, what joy, what freedom.

The other big problem for me was and is, doubt. In college I used to begin my prayers by saying, "God, if you are up there—" and my roommate, who was a good Roman Catholic, would look appalled and say, "Carol, God's going to get you."

If fear has the power to immobilize us and cast us into despair and depression, doubt has the power to suck the zest, the value, and the joy out of life. In the scripture today the disciples are hiding in fear behind closed doors and they are also beginning to doubt. Perhaps Jesus wasn't the one. Perhaps they had been blinded by the charisma of an ordinary man? Perhaps they shouldn't have believed their intuition. Perhaps they were just stupid and easily misled. Do you see the power of doubt. When doubt sneaks into your life you not only begin to doubt God, but you begin to doubt other people, and you begin to doubt yourself.

My divorce was a slow, grinding, painful process that filled me with doubt and led me to believe that all men were scum. My ex-husband had once predicted that I would be a boring, bitter, lonely woman, and part of me believed him. I remember my surprise the day that my future husband walked into my office and asked me out for supper. I'm not sure of the exact look on my face, but he immediately took my look for no, and retreated to his office with a "Never mind." Now that could have been the end of the story, because we were both afflicted by doubt, and in that one short interchange there were several misunderstandings.

First, when he said supper, he meant lunch, which would have been acceptable to me, but supper in my family meant dinner, at night, a big deal, definitely too scary; but I was already past that, to wondering how I could juggle my schedule to be able to accept his invitation. He on the other hand, when he saw my hesitation and indecision, decided that I was trying to find a graceful way to say no and make it easy for me by withdrawing his invitation.

Now Carl is a tall, straight, powerful, imposing man—definitely not someone I wanted to get mixed up with, and yet, I experienced him as fair, understanding, considerate; and others who worked for and with him, loved and respected him. The question was, would I let pain, fear, doubt, anger and past hurt determine my future. I decided that the worst that could happen was that he would think me a fool, and I would feel stupid. But perhaps it was worth the risk. Perhaps what people said about him was true. So I gathered my courage and went in to check out what I thought had just transpired.

That memory of how doubt and fear might have kept us from checking out the meaning behind the words and actions, has kept us out of many, many fights. Now when I get my dander up over some perceived slight or slam, I usually remember to hold my tongue until I have checked it out. It still is amazing to me how my words or body language can be so misunderstood by other people when I think I am being so perfectly clear and intuitive.

Fear and doubt are very powerful. They can make individuals and families so ashamed or afraid of ridicule that small mistakes and sins get shut away in the dark, secret closets where they grow and destroy our self confidence.

Thomas, like Peter, let his pride, or shame, or fear, or doubt pull him out of the fellowship. And so, he wasn't there when Jesus first appeared. When the disciples came to tell him the good news, he was almost belligerent in his pessimism, "Unless I see the mark of the nails on his hands, unless I put my finger into the place where the nails were, and my hand into his side; I will not believe it."

When tragedy or pain or disappointment enter my life I often slip into doubt and disbelief.

Sometimes I react like Peter and deny God, sometimes like Thomas, and my doubt turns into childish rebellion. More than once I have shaken my fist at God and said, "I don't believe in a God who would allow this to happen. Why don't you do something if you are really all powerful." And into that pain, anger and guilt comes the Christ event. "Peace be with you." I have learned that just as Jesus respected Thomas's need and doubt, so too Christ respects and understands our need, our doubt, and fear. I am often hesitant to tell of my experiences of Christ's presence, because they are, well, unbelievable. And besides if I tell you, you might think I am a real certified nut.

When Jesus called the disciples, he did not say he would protect them, he did not promise them an easy life, in fact, just the opposite.

Peace be with you is connected to the pierced hands and side. Peace comes in discovering the true priorities in life. That suffering and death cannot destroy the things of importance, and the threat of suffering and death cannot hold us captive or keep us locked up in boxes of doubt and fear.

It is the peace of Christ's presence that comes in the midst of pain and fear, the peace of Christ's forgiveness that comes in the midst of denial and doubt, that develops faith. It is faith that gives us the courage to make decisions based on God's promises. Faith allows us to open our hearts to God and to one another knowing that rejection, doubt, and fear will not destroy us.

Faith is not something we can claim, or store in a box, or get out of a book—not even the Bible. Faith is a decision to act and react "as if" God's promises were true, "as if" God loves us, "as if" God was always wanting the best for us. Faith is a decision to act "as if" even when we are weighed down with doubt and fear. Faith is a decision that we have to make and keep making every minute, every hour, every day, until that day when our fear and doubt is dissolved and we can say with confidence, "I Believe."

Easter 3   Luke 24:13-35

Recognizing The Risen Christ

Jane H. Rowe

My sister is a school psychologist. It is her job to work with children who are having serious trouble in school, whether academically or in relationships with teachers or with other students. Some of the children she works with come from extremely troubled homes. These children's parents are often so damaged by their own childhoods and so overwhelmed by the demands of life that they take out their frustration and anger on their children. The dysfunction in this primary parent-child relationship lies at the heart of the child's problems in school.

In working with such children, my sister's first task is to work with the child one-on-one. Her approach is not to sit the child down on the psychiatrist's couch and ask questions, but to let the child play while she watches, listens, and asks questions. She learns a lot in this manner, and over a period of time is often able to help the child find some better methods for dealing with the emotions that are causing the troubling behavior. But while the child may be able to function differently in her office, my sister knows that real change will not happen until the relationship between the parents and the child changes. So eventually she may invite one or both parents to be part of the therapy sessions. She asks the parents to do much as she has done—to let the child play or draw, or do something else while the parents look and listen and ask questions and offer encouraging remarks. She wants the parents to see the child with new eyes, to see his or her strengths and potential. But, too often, the parents don't watch and listen. Instead, they talk, pointing out what the child is doing wrong, looking only for something to criticize rather than anything to praise. Quickly the child is acting out in the old familiar ways. Nothing has changed.

This pattern is not only found in extremely dysfunctional families. Many of us get stuck in our relationships with our children, parents, spouses, brothers or sisters. We get stuck in a certain role, a certain way of relating that nobody likes but which is very hard to change. It's hard to stop talking and listen, when what we really want to do is convince the other person that we are right. It's hard to offer encouragement and support when all we can think about is how much better it would be if our loved one would only do it our way. It's hard to see change, growth, and possibility in the person we love when we are preoccupied with all the ways he or she has disappointed us. New life may very well be springing up before our eyes, but unless we stop to look and listen, we shall miss that resurrection moment.

The two disciples walking on the road to Emmaus almost missed the resurrection that was right in front of their eyes, and for much the same reason: they were so focused on their disappointment about who Jesus was not, that they almost failed to see who he really was. They had left the group of Jesus' closest friends and gone off walking by themselves. After all that had happened in the last three days, their heads were surely spinning; they needed to sort things out, to wonder what they'd seen and heard and try to make sense of it. As they walked and talked, a stranger came along, one who seemed to know nothing about the startling events of the last few days. Tears of bitter disappointment shone in their eyes as they told him the story of

Jesus—what a powerful and promising person he had been, and how they had hoped he was the Messiah who, at last, would set Israel free from its enemies, but how those hopes had been dashed as he had been crucified like a common criminal. Even reports of an empty tomb and a vision of angels had been unable to lift their spirits; all they knew was that the one in whom they had placed their hope was dead. He was not what they had hoped and dreamed he would be. In that moment, that was all they could see.

But the stranger had some things of his own to say. As they walked together, he talked to them about who the Messiah was really meant to be—not a mighty king who would overcome their enemies by force, but a suffering servant who would redeem Israel by his sacrificial love. He quoted the scriptures of Moses and the prophet. Those same scriptures they had learned as children suddenly sounded different coming from this stranger's mouth. When they reached their destination, they urged him to stay with them for a meal and a good night's sleep. Certainly they were practicing the art of hospitality which was expected in that society, but I believe it was not only for his need but for theirs that they offered. They had listened to his words, and they wanted to hear more. Their hearts were burning within them, and while they did not yet understand why, they knew they did not want him to leave.

It was only then, when they sat down and began to eat, that they understood. There was something very simple, very ordinary about that moment, when the stranger took the bread and said the blessing and broke it. In an instant, they recognized him. No longer was he a stranger; he was their beloved teacher, Jesus. No longer was he their failed leader, dead and buried; he was their risen Lord, the true Messiah. No longer were they despondent followers who had been tragically misled; they were people filled with resurrection hope, who hurried to share the news with their friends. Had they continued wallowing in their tragic disappointment, they might have missed that moment. But they stopped talking long enough to listen, their hearts burning within them at what they heard. They stopped crying long enough to look, seeing beneath his actions to their deeper significance. It was because they looked and because they listened that these two disciples saw something new, and were themselves renewed.

We, too, have opportunities to witness resurrection in our lives if we will only look and listen—not just with our eyes and ears, but with our hearts. The very relationships that have most bitterly disappointed us may be places where God seeks to reveal to us the risen Christ, the hope of new life. It is new life that God brings, not just the return of the old familiar life we lost. New life cannot come until the old has died and we have mourned its loss. Relationships cannot be reborn until we let go of our need to create the other person in our image and instead allow her or his own unique personhood to emerge. But when we are able lovingly to let go, carefully to look and listen, to see and hear with our hearts, then we shall recognize the risen Christ, the reality of resurrection in our relationships with those we love and with ourselves, and we shall be changed.

I close with a story. A man I know has spent many years trying to talk some sense into his son's head. The man is a brilliant research scientist, and he has great aspirations for his son. The son, now a college student, is a very bright young man with many abilities. But what he wants more than anything is to be a rock musician. You can imagine the father's horror at the prospect. There's no stability in the life of the musician. Except for those who reach the top, there's precious little money in it, and what lasting contribution of real worth can his son ever hope to leave the world, even if he becomes a famous rock star? The father has spent a lot of hours arguing with his son about the mistakes he is sure he's making, and all he has succeeded in doing is driving his son further away. What should he do? Not being a parent myself, it would be presumptuous of me to suggest that I know. I share his concern about his son's choices. But one thing is sure; if the father continues to try to mold his son into a person he thinks he should be, he will most certainly lose the gift of who his son is. Focusing only on his disappointment will prevent him from recognizing the possibilities for life, new life, that are there in his son and in their relationship. He may keep his preoccupation with his son's pursuits of what he believes are dead ends, or he may open his eyes and ears and heart to the potential for hope and life and joy that may emerge in that young man's life. I hope he will choose the way of hope and possibility, for that is the way of resurrection life.

May we also keep our eyes and ears and hearts open, that we may recognize the risen Christ in our relationships and in our lives. Amen.

Easter 4   1 Peter 2:19-25

Suffering, Martyrdom, And The Cross

Allison Stokes

On Sunday, April 18th, 1993, our   congregation joined other congregations in observing Yom Ha Shoah, a day of remembrance of the Holocaust. Our heads and hearts were full of images of bodies burning, of the crematoria in Hitler's Europe, when on the next day, April 19th, we watched the Branch Davidian compound in Waco, Texas, go up in flames, consuming all the people inside.

Some watched tapes of the tragedy on the evening news that night or in the days that followed. Others were alerted, as I was, to the event at the time it was occurring—just after one, Monday afternoon—and we watched the horror live on television, CNN from Waco.

In the aftermath of the event the news reports, the investigation, talk of responsibility and irresponsibility seemed endless. Yet one commentator expressed surprise at the lack of commentary by theologians. What did they have to say about David Koresh? And so on the morning when our scripture lesson lifts up Christ's suffering as exemplary, I address the subject. People of faith need to look at the Waco tragedy and learn from it. What can be said?

First, that David Koresh was a believer whose authority was the Bible. Many of course, consider him to be a nut, the "Wacko from Waco." Others said that this was exactly the problem: the authorities treated him as one mentally ill and failed to recognize or understand his religious commitment, fanatic though it was. We know from his followers that he was deeply steeped in scripture. He would lecture them for hours, quoting from the Bible all the while. The Bible—and particularly the last book, the apocalyptic book of Revelation—was Koresh's source. The image of the compound burning, Koresh's fixation on fire, sticks in our mind, and interweaving with that the images of the holocaust.

On Sunday morning, April 18th, we learned that "Holocaust" or in Hebrew "Shoah" means "burnt offering." On Monday afternoon, April 19th we watched as Koresh burned up himself, his children, his followers as a burnt offering, all the while "following the Bible." I can't help but make the connection with Bible-reading Christians who murdered Jews because the "Jews killed Jesus." Only in recent years are Christians beginning to assume responsibility for the anti-Semitism which has brought untold suffering, destruction, and death to our world. Christians are coming to terms with the destructive ways we have interpreted the Biblical story of Jesus' death. The Jews killed Jesus, we've claimed in the past. It says so in the Bible.

Today we interpret the story differently. We no longer scapegoat the Jews for the death of Jesus. And we apologize for ways we've misused scripture in the name of God. In a kind of parallel way, the tragedy in Waco can prompt us to reinterpret the meaning of Jesus' suffering on the cross. I will explain what I mean in a moment.

To review, my first point was that David Koresh was a believer whose authority was the Bible. My second point is that Koresh apparently thought he was Jesus Christ. His model was a

Christ who suffered and died in obedience to the will of God. Apparently David Koresh thought that to be faithful, his own death and that of his followers and children, was required by God. Human sacrifice was God's will.

However misguided, sick, or appalling we may find this, still we must come to terms with the fact that for 2,000 years, twenty centuries, Christians have interpreted Jesus' death on the cross to be God's will. Jesus' suffering was part of God's plan of redemption. Jesus' death was to save us, and therefore necessary. We say that Jesus was obedient "even unto death." "Obedient"—therefore doing God's will.

There are, however, many Christians who reject this interpretation of the meaning of the cross. Increasing numbers of Bible believers today are reading the story differently. The image of the Branch Davidian compound going up in flames, claiming lives, can push us to examine our own understanding of the cross.

Do we believe in a God who wanted Jesus to die on the cross? Who demanded that Jesus be obedient unto death? Do we believe in a death-dealing God? Or do we believe in a God of life? A God who suffered **with** Jesus on the cross? A God whose answer to human death-dealing is the resurrection, eternal life?

Many Christians today—and you might ask yourself if you are one—reject the doctrine of the atonement, the doctrine that says Jesus was sacrificed for our sins. They remember that when Abraham took his son out into the desert and put him on an altar to sacrifice him, God stopped him. That was a turning point for humanity. God made it known to Abraham that human sacrifice is NOT required. The God of the Hebrew scriptures says clearly, "I set before you life and death, blessing and curse. Therefore, choose life."

Last week in celebration of Earth Day we worshipped outdoors, surrounded by creation, signs of spring and new life all about us. We felt joyful. We are drawn to expressions of Native American spirituality. Native Americans celebrate LIFE.

A friend once asked me "How can you wear that cross all the time? The cross was an instrument of torture, you know." A symbol of violence and death, yes. If that's all it were, I couldn't wear it. But the empty cross is a symbol of resurrection, of Jesus risen from the dead, of life eternal.

I am one of those believers who want to take a hard look at our interpretation of the passion story. What does Jesus' suffering and death mean if it wasn't the will of a God of life? Why did he die?

To give us all something to think about, I want to read from the work of contemporary theologian Beverly Harrison. This is one response to the question, why did Jesus die?

> Orthodox Christological interpretations imply that somehow the entire meaning of Jesus' life and work is to be found in his headlong race toward Golgotha, toward crucifixion—as if he sought suffering as an end in itself to complete the resolution of the divine human drama once and for all. I believe that this way of viewing Jesus' work robs it of its—and his—moral radicality. Jesus was radical not in his lust for sacrifice but in his power of mutuality. Jesus' death on a cross, his sacrifice, was not an abstract exercise in moral virtue. His death was the price he paid for refusing to abandon the radical activity of love—of expressing solidarity and reciprocity with the excluded ones

in his community. Sacrifice, I submit, is not a central moral goal or virtue in the Christian life. Radical acts of love—expressing human solidarity and bringing mutual relationship to life—are the central virtues of the Christian moral life. That we have turned sacrifice into a moral virtue has deeply confused the Christian moral tradition.[2]

David Koresh was one who was deeply confused about sacrifice. His confusion had tragic consequence. One always looks for ways to redeem tragedies. If Christians can become more clear about how we understand Jesus' death, if we can be more clear that God is a God of life, the holocaust in Waco will not have been in vain.

Easter 5 John 14:1-14

What Does Your Heaven Look Like?

Lois Rose

"In my Father's house there are many dwelling places . . . and you know the way to the place where I am going."

This a familiar passage. Because of its familiarity we are in danger of not truly hearing it. Why is it so familiar? Because it is read at many funerals, and even those who don't go to church very often, go to funerals.

Of course, you've probably heard it in the King James version. "In my Father's house are many mansions . . . " that line always intrigued me as a child. I thought there was some great mystery in the saying and my mental picture was of a rather ordinary six room house that in some miraculous way contained many large stately mansions, like English estate houses, or even castles. From the outside it would look just like a regular house, and you wouldn't know that magnificent architecture was hidden inside until you entered the door. This image was my version of seeing the universe in a drop of water and was one of the hooks that got me more and more into the church. Imagine my disappointment when I found out it was just one example of the definition changes that occurred between Renaissance English and modern English for which the King James Version is so famous. I still want my mansion!

In Greek, the word *mon-e*, translated as "dwelling place" is not a common word for room or for dwelling place. It seems to indicate more of a state of being than a place. And there's a transient quality to it, more like "station" as in the stations of the cross, or even a railroad station. Jesus, later in the same chapter, talks of how he and the Father will come to the believer and make a "station" (*mon-e*) with them. (14:23)

In any case, the "household" of God which contains these rooms has usually been interpreted to be an image of heaven. And the idea of heaven has been seen in two ways. The first is the literal state we enter after we die. The second is the description of life on earth experienced in spiritual communion with God, always somewhat incomplete. The two ideas of heaven are both important. Some people believe more in one than the other, but most have some ideas about both, heaven on earth being a foretaste of that which is to come. The two are certainly intertwined in some way, and as we explore here on earth the various kinds of heavenly states, are we not exploring some of the "rooms" or "stations" which may await us?

It seems to me that it matters a great deal what your heaven looks like, as it affects how you see your relationship with God in this life. So I'm going to give you a little test. All of these are heavens that have been described by Christian believers at one time or another. Remember, these are human concepts. Jesus did not give us a blueprint of heaven.

Pay attention now. What does your heaven look like?

1. Is it warm and comfortable with a ready supply of delicious food? And as you enter, does your body become that of a healthy twelve year old? And does God, the loving father or mother, take care of you?

You may smile at the naiveté of this image, but for the person who's life contains large amounts of hunger, cold and

physical pain, this could be heaven. "I'm going to sit at the welcome table" goes the spiritual and one can only imagine the
longing for good food the tired slave brought to this vision.
And, if we are completely honest, we've all felt this way at
times. The problem is that if this remains your only view of
heaven even when you are not hungry or in pain, you will not
hear the cries of the hungry or hurting around you. You will re-
main a perpetual child.

2. Or is your heaven a place of perfect justice? You are safe
from pain and/or humiliation and you can see that those who
caused you or anyone else pain or humiliation are being justly
punished in a place of torment that you can check on periodi-
cally through a television monitor.

This heaven represents, peace, security and absolute justice.
"I'm going to tell God how you treat me," goes the next verse
of the spiritual. "All my enemies shall be ashamed and struck
with terror," says the psalmist (Ps. 6:10). For it is also the
heaven of revenge, the heaven with its counterpart in hell. The
longing for justice is an essential part of a spiritual life, but if
this remains our only view of heaven, life and death can be
dominated by a hunger for power and revenge.

3. Or is your heaven a place of infinite love, where you are
fully accepted and loved, and dare to love freely in return;
where all your loved ones are gathered, and love is the purpose
and end of eternal life?

This is the heaven for those who work hard all their lives at
forgiving and being forgiven. This is the heaven for caretakers
and community builders where all love that is given comes back
manyfold. Obviously, this is one of the central themes of the
Gospel, the good news of God's love for us and of Jesus'

example of love and acceptance. "I'm going to walk and talk with Jesus", goes another verse of the spiritual. This is a great heaven, but if you stay there too long, what do you make of your gifts? For God has given us all many gifts, capable of furthering heaven on earth.

4. Perhaps your heaven is a place where you can develop your gifts, where there is opportunity for giving to others, and where you are esteemed by God and everyone else for your accomplishments.

This is the heaven of the doer, the Jameses and Johns of the world who live the good life of faith, but who would secretly like to sit at the right hand of God, and be given an important job to do. These people work hard for the realm of God, and don't need too much in return. Their motives are, by and large, pure, and they accomplish much. But they are not totally without self-interest.

These are the four heavens that most of us harbor in our souls. We visit each of them on occasion. Some of us hunker down in one or another through most of our lives. They all teach us something, and they all have temptations attached.

However, there are at least three more heavens. They are described in the literature of creative artists and mystics. They go beyond ordinary human desires and goals.

5. The heaven of harmony, freedom, and creativity—could that be your longing? This is the heaven we might call "Eden." It is the heaven where you live fully in the moment, with a lack of self-consciousness. It is the heaven of true creativity for its own sake, and of spontaneous, loving goodwill toward all creation.

6. For some, heaven is the moment or state of total under-standing, when all is known, when our souls cries out a loud "YES." It all makes sense at last.

This heaven is also glimpsed at moments by some. This heaven is the goal of many seekers.

7. And finally, could your heaven be perfect union with God and all creation and full participation in Truth and Beauty? Even if you were to lose consciousness of your self and your identity forever?

Some of the mystics have hinted at this heaven, but it is so far beyond our imagination most of the time.

"Where is my dwelling place?" asks the mystic Angelus Silesius.

"Where stands nor I nor thou." comes the answer.

"Where is my final end, to which I need must go?"

"It is where no end is."

"Then whither shall I press?"

"On even beyond God, into a wilderness."

"In my father's house there are many dwelling places," says Jesus " . . . and you know the way to the place where I am going."

So let us hold onto our visions of heaven, all of them. For even at that moment when the only heaven we can see is the banquet table to which we will walk with a straight back and sturdy legs—even then it is our witness that the veil between the known world and the unseen world is thin indeed. So let us make them "stations" in our lives, not thinking of one as supe-rior to the others, but by participating in all, we allow each vi-sion of heaven to purify the others.

Easter 6   Acts 17:22-31
                                            John 14:15-21

Manifest In Us

Andrea Lasonde Anastos

"In that day you will know that I am in my Father, and you in me, and I in you."

This is not the easiest verse in the gospels to understand, but Paul's sermon to the Athenians in Acts can be profoundly helpful in the process. For most of us, our worship from earliest childhood has been in "shrines made by people" and at altars to "the unknown God." Our knowledge of God has been shaped by the stories we heard as children, by the forms and rituals of Sunday morning and other holy days, by the metaphors created by artists, composers, writers and theologians. Our images of God are external—made for us by other people, rather than internal—direct revelation.

Paul, preaching in Athens, is consumed by the mission that came to him following his experience on the road to Damascus; a mission to bear witness to the one who reveals God to us directly in a form we can see and touch and love. Paul has the audacity to ask us to see and touch and love that no-longer-unknown God in person, face to face.

"In that day you will know that I am in my Father, and you in me, and I in you."

This text comes from the story of the Last Supper and from Jesus' final words to his disciples. With good reason, the disciples are frightened of what is coming, especially since they cannot quite bring themselves to accept the finality of it. Jesus speaks to their fear tenderly by promising them (and all the generations to come, even us), that they will never be alone. He assures them that whatever happens, the *parakletos* will be with them.

In Greece, a *parakletos* was one who supported a person in trouble; the *parakletos* was the one who was called in as an advocate or witness, as a counselor and guide, one who would encourage and inspire. Therefore, Jesus asks us to believe the good news that we have a wise companion through whatever lies before us. His promise is not that this guide will be an intellectual abstraction (a shadowy conscience), but that she will touch our whole beings as Jesus himself touched our whole being: body, mind, spirit, and heart. She will be our friend and we will know her directly.

Then, Jesus promises that he and God will be with us while we are engaged in two acts. First, God is present in our obedience, in the keeping of the commandments. Obedience is a much misunderstood and much maligned concept today. The word "obedience" comes from the Latin: *ob-audire*, meaning to listen attentively to someone. It implies a willingness to listen not only with the ears, but with the heart. Obedience is an act of voluntary **and thoughtful** submission. It is an act that accepts full responsibility. The Spirit will enable us to hear the word of God and the word of the commandments clearly and will lend us strength to follow that way, but the choice to obey is always freely ours. Our obedience means nothing if it is mindless or rote behavior for which we take no responsibility and in which we have no joy. On the other hand, an eager and responsible obedience will put us in a place where we can know God.

The second act through which we meet God is the act of loving. For John, as for Jesus, obedience and love are cause and effect. Love is not an emotion, it is a ministry. Love is a set of choices; sometimes hard, yes, but often exceedingly joyous. Love is not mushy or wishy-washy. Love is a willingness to enter into another's heart and be present for another's needs. Love is not colluding with someone in unhealthy desires (it is not co-dependence). Rather, it is holding firm to the commandments and doing them with every fibre of our being in order that we can be deeply enough rooted to support the weight of another or to feed another from our fullness.

Jesus promises that we will meet God in these three ways: through the guidance of the Holy Spirit, through obedience, and through love. Jesus gives us that promise directly from God and God has never yet broken a promise to humanity. But we need to be willing to name what happens when we obey in love **as God**. We need to be willing to accept that God is fulfilling that promise to us **every day**.

We wonder why Jacob saw angels and we don't. We wonder why Hagar heard God and we haven't. We don't understand that the difference between Hagar and us is not a presence of God in her life and an absence in ours; it is that she was willing to believe God's promise and name God in the small miracles. We, on the other hand, often seem willing only to accept God in God's majestic form: as a whirlwind in Job or as the pillar of cloud or fire at the Exodus. We are not willing to become as little children who see miracles in the unending and unfolding wonder of life itself, in the very **fact** of life.

"In that day you will know that I am in my Father, and you in me, and I in you."

We cannot accept that we will know God exactly as God promised and exactly as Jesus and Paul taught: in the small acts of obedience and love, in the free submission to the guidance of the Holy Spirit touching our hearts and minds, our bodies and souls, in the intimacy of our own spirits and in the souls who sit beside us in the pew or in the bus station.

Little things don't get much attention in the world outside the doors of a church. They aren't considered miracles by most people. A miracle is only something as big as the sun stopping in the heavens. God is only present if we see a towering figure with wings and a crown floating in the sky over Greenfield. (And how many of us would believe even that?) It is a victory indeed for Evil when we relinquish the power of God in us; when we buy into the belief that nothing we see or do qualifies as a miracle!

But God has promised that what we do matters. God has promised that we will know God in the daily moments of commitment to the divine call in our lives. Yes, it is a miracle if the sun stops in the heavens, but it is also a miracle when a family destroyed by alcohol is once again whole. It is new life. The daily denial of desire by the recovering alcoholic, the daily commitment to stay sober for this twenty-four hours, is a miracle. It is obedience and love. And God is present.

It is a miracle when women as busy with work and family as most of our parishioners are, can find the time to cook casseroles and desserts and make salads to feed the hungry in the next town. That is obedience and love. And God is present.

It is a miracle that year after year there are people willing to teach in our Sunday school so that we can hand on to our children the traditions and the stories through which we come to know God. That is obedience and love. It is a miracle when we take a deep breath and count to ten rather than lashing back with the hurtful word when someone angers us. That is obedience and love in action. It is a miracle when we care for an ailing parent or spouse or friend or sibling or child, when we visit them in the hospital or nursing home, when we find a smile when we think we are too tired to keep our eyes open. God is there in the obedience and love. Not in some abstract, nebulous, "spiritual" way, but tangibly. God is there **in us**, manifest in us, incarnate, **real**.

"In that day you will know that I am in my Father, and you in me, and I in you."

Those words of Jesus' mean something. They are a promise for all time.

You are God's children and the power of God is in you in your obedience and in your love. You are important and what you do matters. Take courage, my friends, and take the time to name your obedience and your love with God's name because they are God's miracles—not the unknown God, but God incarnate, God in you. Amen and amen.

Easter 7   1 Peter 4:12-14; 5:6-11

Humility, Pride And Self Esteem

Allison Stokes

In the weeks since Easter many of our scripture lessons center on the theme of how to be Christians in the world, of how, as Christians, we behave rightly. Our lesson this morning, as for the past three Sunday mornings, is from the first letter of Peter, written to Gentile converts to Christianity. In the passage Peter quotes from the book of Proverbs in the Hebrew scriptures: "Clothe yourselves, all of you, with humility toward one another, for 'God opposes the proud, but gives grace to the humble.'"

Humility is not natural to anyone. It must, like clothing, be put on. To raise children in the Christian virtues parents, preachers, and teachers have for many centuries relied on aphorisms in the book of Proverbs:

> Train up a child in the way he should go: and when he is old, he will not depart from it (22:6).

> Correct thy son, and he shall give thee rest; yea he shall give delight unto thy soul (29:17).

> My son, despise not the chastening of the Lord; neither be weary of his correction: for whom the Lord loveth he correcteth; even as a father the son in whom he delighteth (3:11-12).

What I want to talk about this morning is the reliance of parents on corporeal punishment. i.e. bodily or physical punishment as a means of discipline. I'm talking about spanking kids, hitting kids, striking kids. For centuries American parents have been using corporeal punishment in the name of the Bible. Christian parents and preachers have quoted Proverbs:

> Chasten thy son while there is hope, and let not thy soul spare for his crying (19:18)

> He that spareth his rod hateth his son; but he that loveth him chasteneth him betimes (13:24)

> Foolishness is bound in the heart of a child; but the rod of correction shall drive wisdom; but a child left to himself bringeth his mother to shame (29:15)

> The rod and reproof give wisdom; but a child left to himself bringeth his mother shame (29:15)

> Withhold not correction from the child: for if thou beatest him with the rod, he shall not die. Thou shalt beat him with the rod, and shalt deliver his soul from hell (23:13-14)

The rod—a small, straight stick—is to be used to "chastise" or punish bodily. The idea, as you may well know from your own experience of punishment as a child, or from your punishment of your own children, is to teach the child obedience, to break the will of the child. Our foremothers and forefathers believed that this was necessary to bring the child to God. The alternative was an afterlife in hell.

I have been reading a fascinating and important book which talks about the religious roots of corporeal punishment and the psychological impact of physical abuse. It is by Philip Greven, and it is called *Spare The Child*. Greven names and quotes clergy and theologians from the past to the present day who advocate physical punishment. From our own congregational tradition, indeed from our own region of the country, is Jonathan

Edwards. Edwards was obsessed with thoughts of punishment and the tortures of hell. His wife shared his idea. Their grandson wrote about her discipline of her children:

> Her system of discipline was begun at a very early age, and it was her rule, to resist the first, as well as ever subsequent exhibition of temper or disobedience in the child, however young, until its will was brought into submission to the will of its parents; wisely reflecting, that until a child will obey his parents, he can never be brought to obey God.[3]

The methods of discipline are explained in detail by the Edwards' daughter Esther, when she writes about her firstborn child Sally in a letter to a friend:

> I had almost forgot to tell you that I have begun to govourn Sally. She has been Whip'd once on old Adams account, and she knows the difference between a smile and a frown as well as I do. When she has done any thing that she Surspects is wrong, will look with concern to see what Mama says, and if I only knit my brow she will cry till I smile . . . [4]

At the time Esther wrote this letter, her daughter, Sally, was ten months old.

Physical discipline of children is very prevalent in our society. It is not only accepted, but advocated. I read from a "Dear Abby" letter in our local newspaper:

> Just look at the children of today. They need more discipline than just a good "talking to." When I was young, I talked back to mother just once, and I was promptly backhanded across the face, and I never did it again . . . the only thing my parents agreed upon was disciplining me. I was belted, backhanded and whatever it took to keep me in line . . . I'm not saying kids should get hit every day in the week, but when they deserve it, they should get it—but good Abby replied, "I appreciate your

honesty, but you and I part company when it comes to disciplining a child." [5]

The author of *Spare The Child* points out that there is no place in Jesus' teachings—NONE—that can justify the use of the rod, or striking children. Jesus never advocated any such punishment. Today our consciousness is being raised in our treatment of children, as it is in so many aspects of human life. We are learning about the consequence of physical punishment of kids. Child abuse is a problem we are beginning to be aware of and focus upon. We are beginning to understand the connection between violence in our culture and the physical punishment of children. Children who are subject to spanking, hitting and beating, as adults are often filled with repressed anger and rage, hate and aggression, depression, obsessiveness and rigidity, even paranoia.

After reading this book I cannot help but wonder about the source of conflict in churches. Church fights are common. How much of this is the result of adult behavior conditioned by our treatment as children? It's something to think about. Breaking the will of children, humiliating children, has destructive consequences. And until we understand this we will pass the evil from generation to generation.

Happy healthy children esteem themselves, and self esteem is promoted by non-violent child rearing methods. When we respect the bodily integrity and spiritual integrity of children, we do not strike them. Can you imagine Jesus striking a child? It's unthinkable. We are fortunate to have educational material available to help with non-violent parenting, and yet today, there are Christian leaders who advocate corporeal punishment. These are people who cite the Bible, especially Proverbs. I read just one example. The Rev. Jack Hyles writes in 1972 in *How to Rear Children*:

> The parent who spanks the child keeps him from going to hell. Proverbs 23:14, "Thou shalt beat him with the rod, and shalt deliver his soul from hell." A child who is spanked will be taught that there is a holy God Who punishes sin and wrong. Hence he will learn to heed authority and obey the laws and rules. When he hears the Word of God he will obey what he hears and will accept the Gospel as it is preached The parent has kept his child from hell by teaching him truth that can be learned only by discipline and the use of the rod.[6]

In my opinion, fundamentalists who advocate this are very dangerous people. Adolf Hitler is example enough of the destructive consequence of child abuse. Praise God that in our time we are changing our ideas and recovering our Christian roots in the non-violent teaching of Jesus and in the God of tender love to whom Jesus witnessed.

NOTES

ADVENT AND CHRISTMAS

1   Music by J. Fred Coots. Words by Haven Gillespies. Leo Feist, Inc., 1934.

2   Eric Hoffer, *The True Believer* (New York: Harper & Bros, 1951), 11.

3   Music by Jule Styne. Words by Stephen Sondheim. Norberth Productions, Inc. 1959.

4   *O Holy Night.* Music by Adolph Adam, lyrics by Cappeau de Roque Maure and John S. Dwight.

5   Anonymous.

EPIPHANY

1   Elizabeth Barrett Browning, *Aurora Leigh*, book 1, lines 820-822.

2   Annie Dillard, *Holy The Firm* (New York: Harper & Row, 1977), 59.

3   Kate Marks, *Circle of Song* (Lenox, MA: Full Circle Press, 1993).

4   Originally published in *Let Justice Roll Like Mighty Waters,* United Church of Christ, Office for Church in Society, Cleveland, Ohio, April, 1994.

5   Bernie Siegel, *Peace, Love and Healing* (New York: Harper & Row, 1989), 4.

6   Julie Polter, "Living The Word," *Sojourners* (January 1993)

7   Bruce W. Robbins "UFMCC and NCC: Unity Over Justice?" *Christianity & Crisis* 52 No. 19, (January 4, 1993) 424.

8   Matthew Fox,"The Spiritual Journey Of The Homosexual . . . And Just About Everyone Else" in *A Challenge to Love: Gay and Lesbian Catholics in the Church* (New York: Crossroads, 1984), 189-209.

[9]   Eric Marshall and Stuart Hampel, comp., *More Children's Letters To God.* (New York: Simon & Shuster, Inc, 1967).

[10] Walter Wink. *Engaging The Powers* (Minneapolis: Fortress Press, 1992), 275-276.

[11] Wink, 272.

[12] Frederick Carl Eiselsen, Edwin Lewis and David G. Downer, eds., *The Abingdon Bible Commentary* (New York: Abingdon-Cokesbury Press, 1929), 967.

[13] Hans dieter Betz, *Essays on the Sermon on the Mount* (Philadelphia: Fortress Press, 1985), 21ff.

[14] Michael H. Crosby, *House of Disciples* (New York: Orbis Books, 1988), 192-93.

LENT

[1]   Originally preached in 1991 in Portuguese for a new church start in Maputo, Mozambique.

[2]   Dorothee Soelle, *Suffering* (Philadephia: Fortress,1975).

[3]   Based on a liturgy from the United Church of Christ National Women's Meeting, Milwaukee, Wisconsin, 1984.

EASTER

[1]   Patricia Polacco. *Rechenka's Eggs* (New York: Putnam & Grosset, 1988).

[2]   Beverly Wildung Harrison, "The Power of Anger in the Work of Love," in *Weaving The Visions, New Patterns In Feminist Spirituality*, ed. Judith Paskow and Carrol P. Christ. (San Francisco: Harper, 1989), 222-223.

[3]   Philip Greven, *Spare The Child.* (New York: Alfred A. Knopf, 1991), 21.

[4]   Greven, 21.

[5]   *The Berkshire Eagle*, May 19, 1993.

[6]   Greven, 62.

Text Index for Lectionary Readings

Contributors

Andrea La Sonde Anastos is a graduate of Boston University School for the Arts. She studied at General Theological Seminary and graduated with a Master of Divinity from Harvard Divinity School in 1985. She has served for nine years as co-minister with her husband, Rev. George Anastos, of the First Church of Deerfield, Massachusetts, (UCC/UUA). She is a trained spiritual director, has written extensively, and has been a delegate for seven years to the Consultation on Common Texts. She and her husband have an eight year old daughter.

Susan Boone, after 20+ years working in women's history, threw caution to the winds and entered seminary. She is a recent graduate of Bangor Theological Seminary (1994) and is ordained in the United Church of Christ. She is pastor of the First Congregational Church in Chester, Massachusetts.

Shirlee M. Bromley is currently serving as an interim pastor at The Congregational Church in Belchertown, Massachusetts. She has served two other United Church of Christ parishes, one in East Woodstock, Connecticut, and Greenfield, Massachusetts. She also was a missionary from 1969 to 1973. She received her D.Min. from Hartford Seminary in 1990.

Carole Ann Camp is a dreamer and a visionary. She has traveled extensively in Great Britain searching for stone circles and other ancient monuments. She is committed to ending violence against women, racism, homophobia, and sexism. As an ordained minister in the United Church of Christ, her particular interests are ritual and worship.

Ann Duffy is a graduate of Pittsburgh Theological Seminary (1979) and has served churches in New England and the Pacific Northwest. She is an activist with a passion for social justice and social change. Duffy is presently pastor of Zion United Church of Christ in Greshem, Oregon, a church which celebrates it's diversity of culture. She loves small churches and small towns for their ability to get things done.

Mary Susan Gast is Executive Director of the United Church of Christ's Coordinating Center for Women in Church and Society. Ordained in 1975,

Contributors

she has served as campus minister in Iowa, pastored a rural church and an inner city congregation in Michigan, and was an Associate Conference Minister for Indiana-Kentucky.

Mary E. Giles is Associate Pastor of the First Congregational Church (UCC) in Amherst, Massachusetts, and Chaplain at University of Massachusetts at Amherst through the United Christian Foundation. She is also a former truck driver and junior and senior high school biology teacher.

Virginia Lambert Mason sees herself as shaped for ministry by the experiences of community which enabled her to complete with concurrent full-time job and parenting responsibilities. Extended family, babysitting co-ops, various support groups, and a network of friends taught lifelong lessons about vulnerability, trust, and mutual care.

Karen McArthur was raised in the congregational church in Minnesota and is a graduate of Wellesley College and Harvard Divinity School. She was ordained by the United Church of Christ in 1987 and has served as Pastor of the Meriden Congregational Church in Meriden, New Hampshire, and the First Congregational Church in Amherst, Massachusetts.

Ruth Brandon Minter, has had a varied career in ministry, including ethics professor and pastor in Mozambique; journalism, refugee resettlement and peace and justice ministry in North Carolina; campus ministry in Wisconsin; and Area conference Minister in Washington, D.C. and in the Shenandoah Valley of Virginia. She is ordained in the United Church of Christ, currently serving as an interim senior pastor in Massachusetts.

Mary Clark Moschella has served as pastor of the First Congregational Church (UCC) in Lee, Massachusetts, since 1987. She loves to write, hike, and dance. She graduated from Harvard Divinity School in 1983, and is married to Douglas L. Moschella Clark. They have a son, Ethan, and another child due in May of 1995.

Contributors

Jennifer Phillips has served for seven years as Rector of the Episcopal parish of St. John the Evangelist, Boston, and is about to become Rector of Trinity Parish, St. Louis. She was formerly a hospital chaplain at Dana-Farber Cancer Institute and Brigham and Women's Hospital. Born in England, she came to the U.S. at a young age, and has cherished a lifetime interest in science and medicine. She is a poet, and an author of numerous articles and chapters on AIDS ministry and theology and sexuality.

Nancy Rockwell is Senior Minister of the First Parish in Lincoln, Massachusetts. She was ordained by The Church of the Covenant in Boston and also served The United Parish of Auburndale in Newton, Massachusetts. She holds degrees from Brown, Chicago, and Harvard Universities, lives with a cat name Gideon, loves long walks, country dancing and the movies, writes Christmas pageants and op-ed articles, and still considers herself a city person, even after all these years.

Lois Rose has been a United Church of Christ Minister for 22 years. She is currently also studying Ignatian spirituality. She has recently finished a Bible meditation project which uses words and pictures to meditate with Bible stories (available through Ash Grove Press). She is the mother of three and grandmother of five fascinating human beings.

Jane Rowe has pastored Durand Congregational Church (UCC) outside Rochester, New York, for five years. A graduate of Pacific School of Religion and Oberlin College, she is an accomplished pianist and vocalist. Worship services at Durand are rich in music and fellowship.

Valerie E. Russell is the Executive Director of the United Church of Christ's Office for Church in Society, a position that she has held since January 1992. From 1981 to 1991, Russell was the president of the City Mission Society of Boston. She was the first woman and first layperson to head the 175 year old mission society. She has taught and lectured at Harvard Divinity School, Union Theological Seminary and Yale Divinity School.

Contributors

Frances Ruthven is an ordained minister in the United Church of Christ serving as an intentional interim/supply minister in Western Massachusetts. For twelve years she has worked as a pastor and theological educator in Georgia and North Carolina. She lives with her husband and three year old son in Stockbridge.

Donna Schaper is Associate Conference Minister for the Western Area of the Massachusetts Conference of the United Church of Christ. She has served parishes in New York, Massachusetts, Arizona, and Pennsylvania and was formerly associate chaplain at Yale University. She is married to Warren Goldstein, a history professor, and enjoys her three children, Isaac, Katie, and Jacob, ages eleven and twins nine. Her small farm and large garden make her life very happy.

Barbara Kline Seamon was graduated from Hampshire College (Biochemistry 1976) and Yale Divinity School (1982). She studied pathology at the University of Maryland (1977-78) and medical ethics as a Research Fellow at Yale (1983). She is currently pastor of the Athol (Massachusetts) Congregational Church (UCC). Her special interest is exploring the application of the healing arts in the church today.

Allison Stokes, a pastor/scholar, has Ph.D and M.Div. degrees from Yale. She is an historian of the pastoral care and counseling movement and author of *Ministry After Freud*. Allison has served as college chaplain at Vassar and Yale. Currently she is pastor of the Congregational Church in West Stockbridge, Massachusetts, and Founding Director of the Clergywomen's Interfaith Institute in the Berkshires. She recently spent a sabbatical as a Merrill Fellow at Harvard Divinity School and co-authored *Defecting in Place, Women Taking Responsibility For Their Own Spiritual Lives*.

Carol K. Towley holds ministerial standing in The United Church of Christ and Disciples of Christ. She is a Pastoral Counselor and a Licensed Mental Health Counselor. She has her M.A. in Marriage and Family Therapy, and divides her time between part time ministry and part time inpatient and outpatient therapy.

Contributors

Betsy Waters has completed her M.Div. at Andover Newton Theological School and is awaiting a call to bi-vocational ministry. She is particularly interested in helping churches with organizational development and spiritual growth. Waters is also a licensed educational psychologist and works with school age children. She is the mother of three adolescent sons.